What Qualities Does America Want in a President? or Donald Trump v. Democracy

Competence or Incompetence
Morality or Immorality
Law Abiding or Law Breaking
Honest or Dishonest
Faith-Believer or Faith User
Practices Kindness or Is Angry and Creates Fear
Democracy or Autocracy
Environmental Improvement or Drilling, Polluting, Destroying

C. Truett Baker

Library of Congress Control Number:		2024915099
ISBN:	Hardcover	979-8-3694-2582-4
	Softcover	979-8-3694-2580-0
	eBook	979-8-3694-2581-7

Print information available on the last page.

Rev. date: 08/08/2024

To order additional copies of this book, contact:
Xlibris
844-714-8691
www.Xlibris.com
Orders@Xlibris.com
860670

To my loving wife,

CAROLYN S. (SCOTT) BAKER

1934–2024

whose memory I will eternally cherish

Other Books by C. Truett Baker are

Welcoming the Children: History and Programs of Arizona Baptist Children's Services 1960–2002

Church-State Cooperation without Domination: A New Paradigm for Church-State Relations

How the Fundamentalist Grinch Stole the Southern Baptist Convention

Reflections on the Road of Human Experience: A Collection of Essays for Those in Search of Life's Meaning

CONTENTS

ACKNOWLEDGMENTS

As a Christian, I believe God's Spirit provided the inspiration and guidance for this book.

I have dedicated the book to my wife, Carolyn, who has been a loving supporter during our sixty-eight years together. She suffered with medical problems throughout the writing of this book, but I made her care my priority. When she was able, she assisted me in many ways including editing and encouragement.

We live with our daughter, Sue Baker Kohnke, whose computer knowledge has made it possible to publish this book, and I am so grateful for her technical skills and her patience with me.

We also have three other daughters who live in the larger Phoenix area—Carole, Jan, and Valerie, and they too have been supportive, providing us with meals, errands, and other forms of support. We also have numerous family and friends who have prayed for us and helped us in many ways. I wish I could list them all.

I am grateful for the many authors who have provided me with the information that I have needed to write this book. They include psychiatrists, historians, journalists, social workers and other experts in the field of "Trumpism."

The staff at Xlibris Publishing have always been available, professional, and helpful in every way. Particular recognition is given to Sid Wilson, Michelle Postrano and Emman Villaran and skilled editors. Thank you so much!

INTRODUCTION

These are troubled times in politics, religion, and social order. There has been a gradual erosion in civility, decorum, and public trust in recent years. It did not begin with former president Donald Trump, but he has taken advantage of the decline in mood and national spirit and offered to "Make America Great Again." That feeds into the hopelessness and mistrust felt by so many. Many citizens have believed that institutions have failed them and they are fed the crumbs that the elite have given them. Our nation is divided between the "haves" and the "have-nots," and the "have-nots" have become angry and have threatened to make changes. As an example, we have witnessed the tragic and deadly storming of the capitol, and unfortunately, there are those who believe that, or something worse, will happen again.

You will read little in this book that you did not already know, but I believe you will find the organization very helpful in better seeing the whole ugly picture. Books about the former president possibly exceed those written about any other American president. I have perused or completely read forty-six of the many books written about him. I have one book in my library that supports Donald Trump. The title is *The Trump Century* by Lou Dobbs. It rationalizes or tries to explain away Mr. Trump's many lies and unfavorable behavior.

Trumpism is an authoritarian-dictatorial philosophy that creates its own truth and reality, whose ubiquitous power infects all social systems and every other area of life.

This book is the result of research for several years, in many sources on the subject of the aberrant behavior and language of our former president, Donald Trump. He has demonstrated this during his first and only term of office. The uniqueness of the book is not in its originality (although there is some of that) as scores of writers have expressed their views about the former president and his role in the current tragic crisis. The uniqueness of this book is in arrangement of different comments from writers on a single subject, and my own comments tie the opinions of several writers in a manner that brings unity and reflection on the particular subject, and an occasional belly laugh. There is a bibliography of books and articles at the close of this book which have been some of the resources I have used. There are countless other journal articles and documents, but I have been selective in only listing the most damaging to our democracy and most revealing of Mr. Trump's role in the current crisis.

In spite of the numerous sources that are listed, there are many other sources which have been neglected due to the excessive volume. It is unbelievable the number of printed resources that are available on the subject of the former president. I have tried to be fair and balanced in selecting the most pertinent facts, whatever they may be. Part of the difficulty is that the facts have gone through the filter of individual perceptions with different outcomes.

This book is about the voting options our citizenry is facing in the 2024 election of the president of the United States. The rubble of the Trump presidency can become the grist from which those decisions can be made. Much of the blame for recent losses involve our past president Donald Trump. We will review some of those losses as described by many political voices from the media and from Mr. Trump's family and associates. To those who believe that the problems will dissipate when the former president rides off into the sunset—wrong! Trumpism will remain as long as Americans want it to last. He has filled a need in the lives of those who have felt left out and marginalized.

Very few of our citizens would not admit that changes are in order, even though our Constitution and Bill of Rights allow recourse for injustices. We have suffered serious problems before, but part of the present crisis is different in that we previously have had men and women of integrity and courage that have inspired our citizenry to be at their very best and set the example for character and courage, and who listened to their better angels.

We complain and moan, "Ain't it awful," and Pogo, the comic character, has best captured the spirit of the cause of our problems when he said, "We have met the enemy, and he is us." We have shot ourselves in the foot, which has demonstrated our lack of attention, courage, and obedience to the principles that have made our nation the shining light, long valued in the world. (That light is flickering.)

I hope this book will challenge readers to examine their own values and desires and be a part of a mighty new wave of patriotism, faith, and courage that will wash away the moral filth, cynicism, and hopelessness that has polluted our nation in recent years. I repeat myself, but it must be emphasized that our national problems did not begin with our former president, although he has taken advantage of the angry and apathetic mood that hovers over our disenchanted countrymen. And while we are making new promises about what we are going to do, let us not forget to kick ourselves on our backside for not being more alert, courageous, and for putting up with his nonsense and unbelievably poor behavior and disgusting lack of good presidential management.

Of the books I have written, this one has been more challenging. One reason is the stakes are much higher. Another is that there is already a plethora of printed material on this subject. A third reason is the sensitively of the subject. People in their homes, businesses, and places of worship are reluctant to openly discuss the subject because of its potential for divisiveness and retribution. (Oh, let us be honest. Some of us are just cowards!) So many writers have described the uniqueness and seriousness of these times when our very democracy is threatened. One example is that of Andrew Prokop of Vox Media, who has written:

> American democracy is in grave peril. It is besieged on all sides, the threats culminating so far in Donald Trump's attempt to steal the 2020 presidential election from Joe Biden . . . dark scenarios for the future have been posed . . . One is the threat of stolen elections . . . voter suppression. (Vox.com/22798975/democracy-threats-peril-trump-voting-rights)

I would add two others enablers of our hesitation: fear and intimidation.

I am a Christian and write as well as try to live by those values. However, I respect the religion tradition of others, but I believe all people of faith share in the values and principles upon which this nation was built. I must take this opportunity, unwelcomed by some, to share my disappointment and utter sickness to see many of my Christian brothers and sisters who have denied "the faith of our Fathers" by embracing the ungodly and immoral conduct of our former president. This book is written, and prayerfully submitted, in hopes of encouraging others to return to the Judeo-Christian principles they once embraced in the matter of selecting a president. One tangible way is to write or call your congresspeople and tell them how you feel about the two standards of moral discernment that has arrived along with Mr. Trump. He is being held to a lower standard than the rest of us. And of course, voting is a major step in accomplishing our goals. Where is the justice in holding the former president to a different code of ethics and principles in which you and I are held? Any other citizen would be serving time in prison by this time.

As the time for voting approaches, we need to give serious thought to the qualifications of the candidates. Inside the cover of this book, I have listed some of the opposite options that require a response from every voter. This is a no-brainer for many, but for some it will be a difficult choice. I challenge every voter to give serious thought about the kind of nation, even a world, that we want and the kind of president we want to lead us. For Christians, it should be a matter of prayer and aligning the qualities of each candidate with scriptural standards for godly leadership. I hope you can put party loyalty aside and the advice of family and friends and vote your heartfelt Spirit-led conviction. For others who do not follow a particular spiritual path, I hope you, too, can put aside social and cultural bias and vote what your conscience tells you is right.

HERE, IN SUMMARY, ARE THE DANGERS OF ANOTHER TRUMP PRESIDENCY:

1. The United States president has the ability to begin a nuclear war that could destroy or seriously damage civilization. With his anger and proclivity for impulsive violence, Mr. Trump could do that.
2. By word and example, the former president could impair our democracy leading our country toward an autocracy.
3. Our losses, including unity, clean elections, freedom, integrity and reality are just a few of the blessings, that we now enjoy, will be forever gone.

We must admit our country has problems, but our vote and that of our countrymen will decide the future direction of our democracy and the status of our peace and world-wide reputation.

CHAPTER 1

THE TRUMP FAMILY

This book would make little sense without some description of Donald J. Trump's ancestry. Most of us are reflections of our past and carry DNA that transfers hereditary messages across time to current manifestations reflecting our behavior, the color of our eyes, our moods, and thousands of other characteristics. Environment also plays a vital part in who we are and what we do. Donald Trump was born into a jungle of privilege and could have almost anything he wanted. Nevertheless, he was poverty-stricken in character development. This is why a review of his family background is a mirror into his current mentality and behavior.

Johannes Drumpf (1829–1877)

The Trump family begins in this book with Donald Trump's great grandparents, Johannes Drumpf and Katherina Kober, both from Kallstadt, Germany. This was wine country and the Drumpf family became a part of it, although it was a hard living. The Thirty-Year War was just beginning and involved all of Germany. It "ushered in one of the worst periods in Kallstadt's bloody history. Soldiers emptied their vats of wine several times, but the family survived. The little community was burned down at least five times . . . At one period, only ten families remained" (Trump, Fred: thefamouspeople.com/profiles/fred-trump-11975).

The name Drumpt was changed to Trump during this period. Johannnes was not in good health. He could no longer work in the family fields. Two sons had died in infancy and his brother was killed in a tree-cutting accident. After an illness of ten years, he died on July 6, 1877, at the age of forty-eight. The family was poor but industrious. The children worked in the fields and the small income from the wine-grapes was enough to live on. Nevertheless, they were generous to their Lutheran Church.

Freidrich Trump (1869–1918)

Freidrich, the fourth child of Johannes and Katherina, was born March 14, 1869, in Kallstadt, in the Kingdom of Bavaria. At the age of fourteen, his mother, Katherina, sent him to a barber in a nearby town, Friedrich Lang, who needed an apprentice. Freidrich was too frail to work in the fields as the other children did. For seven days a week, he opened the shop and cleaned the floors. After two and one-half years, he completed his contract and was a professional barber. He returned to his home in Kallstadt in the fall of 1885. His mother could ill afford to feed one more mouth and there was little work for him in cutting hair there. He discussed this with his mother and they agreed he should travel to America and he made plans to leave. One night, he wrote a note to his mother explaining his situation and off to America he went. (Opt. Cit., Blair, pp. 135–137). He was sixteen years old.

Freidrich paid $20 for a place in steerage class aboard the SS *Eider* on October 7, 1885. When he arrived in New York City's Castle Gardens ten days later, he found a place to live with his sister and her husband who had moved there years earlier. Immediately, he went to work at his barber trade the day following his arrival to his new country. He was literate, but in German. Friedrich was finally able to send money back to help his mother. He was patient, but as the years went by, he became tired of the seven-day workweek and his routine at the barber shop, and he was envious of the wealth he saw all around him. He was determined to find a place where somebody with grit and determination could become a rich man fast.

In1891 at the age of twenty-two, he moved to Seattle and began speculating in real estate while also operating the Dairy Restaurant. This was in an area of saloons, casinos and brothels. It was called a hotbed of sex. In 1892, he became a naturalized citizen. Freidrich started his business operating a restaurant/brothel in Seattle. He sold that business and moved to a nearby community and set up a small hotel/brothel taking advantage of the oil-rich area.

Before leaving Seattle, he bought forty acres in the Pine Lake Plateau for $200. This was the first real estate purchased by a Trump family member. He founded his own construction business in partnership with his mother. He was under legal age and could not yet sign legal papers. The mining project didn't materialize and he moved again. He heard of the Klondike gold rush in Canada's Yukon area and moved there. Again, he established a bar and grill called the Artic. It featured liquor and "sporting ladies." After the gold ran out, he had made a small fortune in his business and headed back to Kallstadt.

He believed he had enough money now to get married and settle down. For this important event in 1901, he wanted to find his bride back in Germany. Freidrich's mother was not the least happy about her son's choice of a bride. Although an earlier neighbor, her family was from a lower social class and she could not understand why her son picked Elizabeth Christ out of all the eligible ladies in the town. They were married on August 26, 1902.

Earlier, Freidrich had become a naturalized citizen of the US. After marriage, their plan was to remain in Kallstadt and make their home there. Freidrich applied for reinstatement of German citizenship and was turned down. The government saw his earlier departure from

Germany as a means of avoiding the draft although he denied this. No amount of pursuing this goal was successful. On June 30, 1905, the Freidrich Trump's family left Germany for the last time. Elizabeth was five months pregnant with her next child, Fred Trump, Donald Trump's father.

After their return to America, Freidrich returned to his barbering trade to make a living. He was not content to pursue this career although it had been a wage-earning opportunity several times in his life. By 1906, he found the opportunity he was looking for in the construction business.

Taking advantage of major infrastructure improvements, Freidrich purchased a two-story frame structure in Woodhaven. In addition, he accepted a job as manager at the Medallion Hotel. Other moves were made and the builder was on his way to achieving his goal. One day, he and his oldest son were walking and Freidrich became ill. He died the following day, May 29, 1918.

Friedrich "Fred" C. Trump (1905–1999)

Fred Trump met his future wife, Mary Ann MacLeod, from Scotland at a dance party and they were married January 11, 1936, at the Madison Avenue Presbyterian Church. The couple settled in Jamaica, Queens. They had five children: Maryanne Trump Barry, born in 1937, who became a federal judge; Fred Trump Jr., born in 1938, who became an airline pilot; Elizabeth Trump Grau, born 1942, who became an executive for Chase Manhattan Bank; Donald J. Trump, a realtor, born in 1946, who became the forty-fifth president of the United States; and Robert Trump, born in 1948, who became a top executive in his father's property management company, and later, a commercial pilot.

Fred had been interested in construction most of his young life. After his father died, their financial legacy quickly diminished. Fred was only fifteen years old, and because he was underage to do business, he and his mother, Elizabeth, formed a company which they named E. Trump and Son. He went back to trade school and learned carpentry and to read blueprints. Fred also learned plumbing, electricity, and brick and block installation. He grew up with his elder sister, Elizabeth Trump Walters, and younger brother, John George Trump.

He began by building car garages and then apartments. He built barracks and apartments near the naval base during World War II. He later constructed housing for veterans returning from the war. He built more than 27,000 apartments in and around New York City.

In 1934, Trump and his partner acquired in federal court the mortgage-servicing subsidiary of the Brooklyn's J. Lehrenkrauss Corp., which had gone bankrupt and had been divided up into smaller units for liquidation. This gave Trump access to the titles of many properties nearing foreclosure, which he bought at low cost and sold for a handsome profit. This and other real estate ventures quickly thrust him into the limelight as one of New York City's most successful businessmen. Trump made use of loan subsidies created by the Federal Housing Administration (FHA).

As the children grew, the time gradually came when Fred and Mary talked about their children's future. Mary had hoped that their oldest son, Fred Jr., would continue the family construction business. Neither Fred Sr. nor Fred Jr. embraced the idea with an ounce of enthusiasm. Fred Jr. was more interested in flying. Instead, Fred Sr. selected another son, Donald, to be his successor as head of the family business. He knew of Donald's interest in construction, and while not close during Donald's childhood, their bond strengthened as the partnership came together. Fred Jr. died of alcoholism in 1981 after a successful career as a pilot. Donald joined his father's real estate business in 1968. He became president in 1971. Mary L. Trump, his niece, reported that Fred was intimately involved in every detail of his son's activities, including financing. In mid-1970s, Fred loaned his son in excess of $14 million. Later, Donald claimed it amounted to only $1 million.

All was not roses. Fred faced charges of racial discrimination, which was resolved by consent decrees being signed. Both sides claimed victories. At one point, he was charged with code violations in a 504 unit construction in Maryland. Fred was arrested and released on bond. He could be generous at times. His favorite charities were the Jamaica Hospital Medical Center, United Cerebral Palsy, a home for functionally retarded adults, the National Kidney Foundation and the Long Island Jewish Hospital in Manhattan.

In October 1991, Fred was diagnosed with Alzheimer's disease and died on June 25, 1999, at age of ninety-three. At the time, his estate's value was estimated at around $250 to $300 million. His widow, Mary, died on August 7, 2000, at the age of eighty-eight. Their combined estates were estimated at $51.8 million.

(Much of the above family information is credited to Gwenda Blair's book *The Trumps*. Most of the specific references have been lost in the repeated transfer of information and organization of the book. A Touchstone Simon and Schuster book, New York, 2000, pp. 23–94)

CHAPTER 2

DONALD TRUMP: THE FORTY-FIFTH PRESIDENT OF THE US

Donald John Trump was born in Queens, New York, on June 14, 1946. His ancestors were from Germany and Scotland. He was the fourth of five children born to Fred Trump and Mary McLeod. He was educated at the New York Military Academy and the Wharton School of Finance and Commerce at the University of Pennsylvania.

His first marriage was to Ivana Zelnickova Winklmayr on April 9, 1977. They had three children: Donald Trump Jr., Ivanka M. Trump, and Eric Trump. They were divorced March 22, 1992. Donald J. Trump's second marriage was to Marla Maples on December 20, 1993, in New York City. They divorced June 8, 1999. Their only child was Tiffany Trump born October 13, 1993, in West Palm Beach, Florida. His third and current marriage is to Melania Knauss and they have one son, Barron Trump.

Fred Trump, Donald's Father

Donald J. Trump's father, Friedrich "Fred" C. Trump made his fortune in real estate enabled by government financing. He hated paying taxes, in spite of support from the government. His assets were mostly tied up in property, mainly in Brooklyn and Queens. Early in his career, he lied about his age to appear more intelligent than he was. Like his son, Donald, he used hyperbole expressions, such as great, fantastic, and perfect. Father, Fred, took little interest in the children, unless they did something that made him (Fred) look good.

Donald Trump's mother, Mary, had a serious health problem, but on her better days, she enjoyed a social life, absenting herself from home and the children. Dr. Mary Trump, Donald's only niece and a trained clinical psychologist, has bravely written her uncle Donald's biography. While the family was not especially close, Dr. Trump attended most of the family gatherings and was able to observe Donald's behavior first-hand.

(Note to readers: Dr. Trump's book *Too Much and Never Enough* has a byline under the title which reads, "How My Family Created the World's Most Dangerous Man." I admire her bravery and candor in giving us an inside picture of "the world's most dangerous man." The author has footnoted the information used from her book. However, some of the thoughts and ideas are not so noted.)

As a clinical psychologist, Dr. Trump had the skill to evaluate the family dynamics. She writes, "Whereas Mary was needy, Fred (Donald's father) seemed to have no emotional needs at all . . . He was a high-functioning sociopath . . . Symptoms of sociopathy include a lack of empathy, a facility for lying, and indifference to right and wrong, abusive behavior, and lack of interest in the rights of others . . . As Donald grew older, he suffered deprivations that would scar him for life."

By this time, most readers will begin to see several things. Donald Trump suffered from parental neglect. He didn't receive the guidance, nurturing, and discipline so necessary to normal development. He was enrolled in the prestigious private school, Kew-Forest. His behavior of fighting, bullying, and confrontation with other students, teachers, and staff eventually resulted in his dismissal.

Unfortunately, this behavior didn't bother his father. One of Fred's fellow board members at Donald's school suggested that he send Donald to the New York Military Academy. Donald was unhappy about this decision, but it did bring a measure of discipline and self-control to his unruly behavior. However, his personality and character were firmly entrenched into the sociopathic man he became.

As Donald Trump grew into adulthood, he learned the real estate, hotel, resort, commercial buildings, casino, golf course, and other business ventures from his father who now took more interest in Donald as the torch of business operations was gradually passed to him. Donald was not the businessman he thought he was. At one point, he had bought two casinos in Atlantic City, a yacht for $29 million, Mar-a-Lago for $8 million, and Eastern Airlines Shuttle for $365 million. By 1990, his personal debt grew to $975 million. His father and grandfather bailed him out several times, but he still experienced six bankruptcies. Other priorities included Supreme Court and federal judiciary appointments, taking the opioid epidemic slowly, attempting to lower the cost of prescription drugs and improving health care for veterans.

The banks were in a double bind as the Trumps were one of their best clients and they believed they had to continue funding Donald's failures. Finally, the banks made an agreement with him in May 1990 that "they would put him on a $450,000-a-month allowance—that is almost $5.5 million a year for having failed miserably." In return, Donald had to meet with them weekly to account for his expenditures.

The Art of the Deal and the Apprentice

Trump had been a well-known personality since the eighties and the publication of his first book, *The Art of the Deal*, made him into an icon of American success.

In the summer of 1987, Donald Trump, with the help of a professional writer Tony Schwartz, wrote *The Art of the Deal*. (It was on the *New*

York Times bestseller list for thirteen weeks, and it received very positive reviews.) The book was part autobiography and part business advice. However, literary professionals cast doubt on the accuracy of some of the events in the book. Mr. Trump took all the credit for all the writing of the book much to Mr. Schwartz's disappointment. The publisher Howard Kaminsky said that the former president "played no role in the actual writing of the book." When confronted with this contradiction, Mr. Trump's explanation was that this was a "truthful hyperbole". Later, one of this aids, Kellyanne Conway, explained this seeming contradiction as "alternative facts." (en.wikipedia.org/wiki/ Trump:The_Art_of_the_Deal)

The popularity of this book was a means for introducing Mr. Trump to a huge audience who knew nothing about him previously.

At a low ebb in the former president's business life, a television producer Mark Burnett produced a reality show, *The Apprentice,* and asked Mr. Trump to be his partner and host the show.

The first episode began on January 8, 2004, and the final episode was aired February 13, 2017. Trump was the show's host for the first fourteen seasons and was fired for making inappropriate racial comments in his inaugural address, as the new USA President. Dylan Matthews of VOX Media, captured this situation in the title of an article he wrote, "How Reality Caught Up with the Reality TV President". He and his partner, Mark Burnett, remained friends and planned to work together on other projects. One of the producers, Katherine Walker, told the author of the above article, "But Donald would not be President had it not been for the show."

The Surprise Announcement

When Donald Trump's niece, Mary L. Trump, heard of his announcement to run for the presidency, she wrote in her book about her reaction: "When Donald announced his run for the presidency on

June, 2016, I didn't take it seriously . . . He's a clown . . . This will never happen" (Trump, Mary L., PhD, *Too Much and Never Enough,* Simon and Schuster, 2020, p. 8).

An attorney-author, Sarah Posner, wrote in her book about Donald Trump, *Unholy,* her reaction to the announcement of his presidential candidacy— "I was deeply skeptical that he would be their man" (Posner, Sarah, *Unholy,* Random House, New York, 2020, p. xiii). Dr. Posner is a reporting fellow with Type Investigations who had traveled to seventeen states gathering information from many sources about Trump's campaign.

Ben Howe, writer, podcaster, and filmmaker, has appeared as a commentator on CNN and MSNBC and is the author of *The Immoral Majority.* He wrote in his book, "In the summer of 2016 the idea that the real estate mogul and reality television star Donald Trump might actually become president was utterly laughable to most experts, pundits, and the Washington power structure . . . He was at once the carnival barker and the sideshow being barked" (Howe, Ben, *The Immoral Majority,* Broadside Books, New York, 2019, p. 1). (The barking never seemed to get out of his repertoire of deceit.)

His nomination for president in 2016 was seen as a joke by some and a long shot by many. The campaign was divisive, negative, and controversial in the areas of qualification for office, immigration, and race. He was only the fifth presidential candidate in US history to lose the popular vote but win the electoral vote, which decided the election. Trump lost the popular vote by 2.87 million and received 304 electoral votes winning over Mrs. Clinton's 227 electoral votes.

The four-year term as president was unusual, chaotic, and severely divided the nation. His language was often invidious, crude, and demeaning. He embraced our foreign enemies and alienated our allies. The changing of his cabinet members and other staff was record-breaking. He gave new meaning to the cliché, "It's my way or the highway." The "highway" was very busy.

He courted the Religious Right and charmed the Christian population beyond belief. Kristin Kobes Du Mez, professor of history at Calvin University and frequent contributor to *Christianity Today, Christian Century,* the *Washington Post,* and *Religion and Politics,* has written *Jesus and John Wayne: How White Evangelicals Corrupted a Faith and Fractured a Nation.* On the first page, she describes Mr. Trump's speech at a small Christian college in Iowa in January 2016. In embellishing the strength of his following, he stated, "I could stand in the middle of Fifth Avenue and shoot somebody and I wouldn't lose any votes" (Du Mez, Kristin K., *Jesus and John Wayne,* Liveright Publishing Corp., New York, 2020, p.1).

The same professor described the following in the second paragraph of her book, continuing the account of the event at the Iowa Christian college:

> That morning, the Reverend Robert Jeffress, pastor of First Baptist Church, Dallas, Texas, introduced Trump . . . He made it clear that he wouldn't be there if he didn't think Trump "would make a great president." Jeffress wasn't alone. Already at that point, before the Iowa caucuses at the beginning of February, 42 percent of white evangels supported Trump—more than any other candidate.

Perhaps his most glaring fault was lying and deceiving. The Fact Checker Staff of the *Washington Post* documented this nefarious activity. From the start of Trump's presidency, the *Washington Post* Fact Checker team has catalogued every false or misleading public statement he has made. As of Jan. 20, 2020, three years after Trump took the oath of office, the count stood at 16,241. That works out to fifteen claims per day. But the pace of deception has quickened exponentially.

Another source describing this man's lack of character and his immorality is recorded in the *Access Hollywood* tapes. On October 7,

2016, the *Washington Post* published a video and accompanying article describing a time he and Billy Bush, a television host, were on a bus on the way to film an episode of *Access Hollywood*. They were, "having an extremely lewd conversation about women in 2005 . . . In the video Trump described his attempt to seduce a married woman and indicated he might start kissing a woman that he and Bush were about to meet . . . I don't even wait. And when you are a star, they let you do it. You can do anything . . . grab'em by the p———."

Trump's Appeal

The question in many minds is how a narcissistic, vulgar, crude, racist, misogynist, lying, hypocritical man with no political or government experience could be supported for president by Christian and non-Christian people alike. One writer expressed his popularity and appeal:

> Even after four years of lying, corruption and incompetence, somewhat damningly close to fifty percent of Americans want Donald Trump to continue lying, corrupting, and "incompetenting." Those people won't go away just because Trump does. And anyway, he won't go away. I'll bet everything I own that he'll continue to erode the already shaky standards of respect, compassion and decency in political discourse from the sidelines. (reference unavailable)

The reasons for this devotion are many and complex, and scholars and pundits alike offer their explanation for this weird and almost macabre new American experience. One writer compares the similarities of Trump with Hitler's motive in seeking power (Haynes, Stephen, "If You Board the Wrong Train," in Sider, Donald (Ed.), *The Spiritual Danger of Donald Trump*, Cascade Books, Eugene, OR, 2020, pp. 110–111).

Another writer posits an unusual but very believable explanation. "The glib way to answer the question is that a certain percentage of the

American public love bigoted demagogues, and that's that." Adding to that, he said, "America has been in love with outlaws since its early days, and leaders like Trump who seem to achieve power while flouting the rules of decorum, exert a kind of magnetic pull" (Ryan, Shane, "Why is Donald Trump So Appealing to So Many People?" *Paste* Magazine, October 22, 2020, pastemagazine.com/politics/donald-trump/donald-trump-so-appealing-to-so-many-people).

The same writer offers another reason for Trump's hold on certain groups. "But on a gut level, Trump also scares them. And that power of inspiring fear is transmitted to his supporters because the ability to scare another person, to control them in that way, has been appealing to human beings forever" (Ibid).

Dr. Mary Trump, Donald's niece, gives her reason for his popularity. "He had a streak of superficial charm, even charisma, that sucked certain people in" (Opt.Cit., Trump, p. 138).

He and his followers share common characteristics with the Religious Right and religious fundamentalism. They share a purpose in "saving" the nation and even the world from dire consequences. The fundamentalists are determined to save the church from liberalism. Mr. Trump would "Make America Great Again," saving it from social and political downfall. Sarah Posner, investigative journalist and attorney, has written in her book *Unholy*, "Trump is no ordinary politician and no ordinary president. He is anointed, chosen, and sanctified by the movement as a divine leader sent by God to save America" (reference unavailable).

Among his many presidential advisors, was wealthy evangelist, Paula White, who advised him on many matters but especially spiritual ones. He heard her preach in the early 2000s and saw where her advice could serve him in several ways both in business and politics. She later bought a condominium in the Trump Tower for $3.5 million dollars. In an interview with James Dobson, founder of Focus on the Family and a strong Trump supporter, he remarked that it was Paula White who led him "to accept a relationship with Jesus Christ." When questioned about his crude language and behavior, those close to Trump would say, "We're all sinners" or "He's still a 'baby' in Christ and growing."

He could not accept losing the bid for a second term as president, claiming that he was the actual winner and the election was stolen from him. That became the big lie and a rallying point for him and his followers to continue to fight for control.

The Campaign Trail

This journey does not begin with Donald Trump's announcement of his decision to run for president while walking down the staircase of the Trump Tower to the press and friends below. Rumors of this possibility had been circulating for years. David Cay Johnson, an author and investigative journalist, who was winner of a 2001 Pulitzer Prize for journalism, *The Making of Donald Trump*, had the following points to make regarding a 2005 speech from Donald Trump in Colorado:

o   For more than an hour, the future president made his points with one four-letter expletive after another.
o   He had no prepared text.
o   He ran down the location and functionality of the Denver International Airport.
o   The rambling remarks were rich with denunciations of former wives and former business associates.
o   In vilifying a former employee, he described her as "ugly as a dog."
o   "I love losers because they make me feel so good about myself."
o   Trump has been a party to 3,500 lawsuits.
o   He recommended as a business policy, "Trust no one, especially good employees."
o   "I can't stomach disloyalty . . . I love to get even when I get screwed by someone."

o "No one reads the Bible more than I do."

o He says his book *The Art of the Deal* is the greatest book ever written, except the Bible (no one has ever heard him quote a verse from the Bible).

Give Credit Where Credit Is Due

It is difficult to recognize any positive achievements of Mr. Trump when so much sleaze, deceit, lying, and violence characterizes his presidency. But in fairness, I believe the major achievements during his watch should be recognized. Keep in mind that some of these achievements had their beginning during the time of earlier presidents. Giving credit to others, particularly victories, is just not a part of his nature. The following are a partial list of those achievements.

1. Reshaping the federal judiciary. Three Supreme Court justices and 220 federal judges were sworn in. (Most, if not all, are Trump supporters.)
2. A sixth branch of the US armed forces, the Space Force, was added after he signed a $738 million defense spending bill.
3. Tax Reform—The biggest overhaul was made to the nation's tax code in three decades. The corporate tax rate was cut to 21 percent from 35 percent.
4. The First Step Act was approved making modest changes in the federal prison system, offering more rehabilitation and job training.
5. The ISIS Caliphate was defeated and the leader, Abu Bakr Baghdadi, was killed.
6. Three bills were passed to benefit Native Americans.
7. President Trump signed a law to make cruelty to animals a federal crime.
8. The president gave $100 million to repair water infrastructure problems in Flint, Michigan. This process began with President Obama.

9. In 2018, the US surpassed Russia and Sadia Arabia to become the world's largest producer of oil. The beginning of this increase predated Mr. Trump.

10. The president signed a bill requiring airports to provide spaces for breast-feeding Moms.

11. The president signed the Save Our Seas bill, which funds $10 million per year to clean tons of plastic and garbage from the ocean.

12. Former President Trump signed an executive order that forces all health care providers to disclose the cost of their services.

13. VA employees are being held accountable for poor performance, with more than 4,000 VA employees removed, demoted, or suspended.

14. Former President Trump issued an executive order requiring the Secretaries of Defense, Homeland Security, and Veteran's Affairs to submit a joint plan to provide veterans access to mental health treatment as they transition to civilian life.

15. Trump signed into law up to twelve weeks of paid parental leave for millions of federal workers.

16. Former President Trump's Department of Health and Human Services provided funding to support the National Human Trafficking Hotline to identify perpetrators and give victims the help they need.

17. The tax cuts signed into law by President Trump promote school choice by allowing families to use 529 college savings plans for elementary education.

18. Former President Trump issued an executive order prohibiting the US government from discriminating against Christians or punishing expressions of faith.

19. Has imposed sanctions on the socialist government in Venezuela who have killed their citizens.

20. Finalized new trade agreement with South Korea.

21. Secured $250 billion in new trade and investment deals in China and $12 billion in Vietnam.

22. Has had over a dozen US hostages freed, including those who Obama could not get freed.
23. Trump signed measures funding prevention program for veteran suicide.
24. Legislation was passed that required able-bodied men without children to work or look for work if they are on welfare. In Arkansas alone, over 18,000 Medicare beneficiaries lost their coverage.
25. NATO allies increased their defense spending because of the pressure put on them by Mr. Trump.
26. Withdrew the US from the job-killing Paris Climate Accord in 2007 and that same year the US still led the world in having the largest reduction in carbon emissions.
27. Was instrumental in having the US Embassy in Israel moved to Jerusalem.
28. The Trump Administration updated the North American Free Trade Agreement, fulfilling a campaign promise.
29. Signed into law the most comprehensive childhood cancer legislation ever, which will advance childhood cancer research and improve treatments.
30. In 2018, former president Trump signed into law $2.4 billion funding increase for the Child Care and Development Fund, providing a total of $8.1 billion to states to fund child care for low-income families.

A List of Books for Which He Claims Authorship

If is doubtful if Mr. Trump actually wrote any of the books listed below that bear his name as author. However, he does give his ghostwriter, Tony Schwartz, credit as "coauthor" of his first book, *Trump: The Art of the Deal*. There are other ghostwriters in addition to Tony Schwartz.

The Art of the Deal by Donald Trump and Tony Schwartz
The Autobiography by multiple writers

The America We Deserve by Donald Trump

My Fellow Americans by Donald Trump

How to Make America Great Again by Donald Trump

America's Greatest Presidents by Donald Trump

Make It Happen in Business and Life, by Donald Trump

Our Journey Together by Donald Trump

The Greatest Speeches of Donald Trump by Donald Trump

How Reasonable Americans Could Support Trump: Helping Liberals Understand the MAGAverse by Brian M. Rees

Trump Tweets by Tony Robson

Time to Get Tough by Donald Trump

Think Like a Champion by Donald Trump

Wealth Building 101 by Donald Trump

Surviving at the Top by Donald Trump

How to Get Rich by Donald Trump

The Beautiful Poetry of Donald Trump by Rob Sears

Great Again by Donald Trump

Winners Aren't Losers by Donald Trump

The Art of the Comeback by Donald Trump and Rob Sears

Think Like a Billionaire by Donald Trump

Why We Want You to Be Rich by Donald Trump and Robert T. Kiyosaki

The Best Golf Advice I Ever Received by Donald Trump

All the President's Women: Donald Trump

How I Turned My Biggest Challenges into Success by Donald Trump

Why Some Entrepreneurs Get Rich-And Why Most Don't by Donald Trump and Robert T. Kiyosaki

CHAPTER 3

THE CHARACTER OF
DONALD TRUMP

He Exploits Religion to Serve His Own Selfish Interest

Religious leaders were flattered that Mr. Trump took an interest in them and the fact that he appeared to support conservative values such as opposing abortion. They were also flattered by the fact that "his door was always open to them." It never seemed to matter to them that his personal life and behavior were a moral disaster. In fact, they even made excuses for such behavior.

The Bible seems to be talking about Mr. Trump when it says, "But mark this: There will be terrible times in the last days. People will be lovers of themselves, lovers of money, boastful, proud, abusive, disobedient to their parents, ungrateful, unholy, without love, unforgiving, slanderous, without self-control, brutal, not lovers of the good, treacherous, rash, conceited, lovers of pleasure rather than lovers of God—having a form of godliness but denying its power. Have nothing to do with such people" (2 Tim. 3:2–5).

Mr. Trump claims to be a Christian, but his language and behavior doesn't support his claims. He actually uses religion to achieve selfish purposes without worshipping God or seeking His will in his life. When questioned about his faith, he replies, "Why do I have to repent or seek God's forgiveness if I am not making mistakes?"

The Bible (who Trump claims to be familiar with) is very clear about cognitive dissidence (hypocrisy)—false believers who are masquerading as saints.

> For such men are false apostles, deceitful workers, disguising themselves as apostles of Christ. And no wonder, for even Satan disguises himself as an angel of light. Therefore, it is not surprising if his servants also disguise themselves as servants of righteousness, whose end shall be according to their deeds. (2 Cor. 11:13–15)

The pro-Trump evangelicals are doing more to damage the Christian witness than the co-called New Atheists ever could.

Fred Trump was Donald Trump's father. He had little use for his children until they were old enough to be involved in the family's real estate empire. Fred's neglect included any religious training. However, he heard about "the prosperity gospel" preached by Norman Vincent Peale in the 1950s and was quite impressed. He read Peale's *The Power of Positive Thinking*, and on that basis, he and his family joined the church, but seldom attended.

Dr. Mary Trump, Donald's niece and interloper author of his biography, described Dr. Peale in her book *Too Much and Never Enough*, "Peale was a charlatan, but he was a charlatan who headed up a rich and powerful church, and he had a message to sell" (Ibid., p. 37). And that message was that if you were positive and believing in a matter, you could make about anything come true.

The Trump family used the church for weddings and funerals, and that about says it all about Donald Trump's relation to religion all of his adult life. After he became president, the Religious Right gravitated to him due to his conservative agenda and access of the religious leadership to the White House.

Before listing religious leaders who support Trump, I want to share a thought from Dr. Stephen R. Hayes, professor of religious studies and director of liberal arts in Prison Program at Rhodes College, where he has taught since 1989. He has heard Trump supporters who try to justify his irreverent language and behavior by saying, "God works through imperfect vessels, particularly if they are engaged in the larger task of 'restoration.'" To this inane comment, Hayes sees a parallel between Hitler and Donald Trump (Opt. Cit., Sider, p. 111). He cites the following examples:

- "No one could welcome January 30, 1933, [the date of Hiler's accession to power] more profoundly or more joyfully that the German Christian leadership."

- "[Hitler is] the best man imaginable, a man shaped in the mold made of unity, piety, energy, and strength of character."

- "[Hitler], the most German man, is also the most faithful, a believing Christian. We know that he begins the day and ends the course of the day with prayer, that he has found in the Gospel the deepest source of his strength."

- "If the German who truly believes in Jesus could find the spirit of the kingdom of God anywhere, he could find it in Adolf Hitler's movement."

- "[God has granted us an] hour of grace . . . through Adolf Hitler."

- "God has once again raised his voice in a singular individual."

Note the similar language used by these American Christians in response to Trump's election:

- "God raised up . . . Donald Trump" (Michael Bachmann).

- "God has righteously chosen [Trump] to affect the way that this nation goes forward" (Chuck Pierce).

- "Donald Trump represents a supernatural answer to prayer" (James Robison).

- "Donald Trump actively seeks God's guidance in his life" (James Dobson).

- Trump's victory "showed clear evidence of 'the hand of God' on the election" (Franklin Graham).

- "[Trump] does look like he's the last hope" (Phyllis Schlafly).

- "God has raised up [Trump] for such a time as this" (Stephen Strang).

- "We thank God every day that he gave us a leader like Donald Trump" (Robert Jeffress)."

"Like those naive and desperate Germans, many of our Christian leaders, convinced that God was at work in Trump's unlikely accession to power, have been willing to interpret whatever Trump says and does as in keeping with the divine plan" (Ibid., pp. 111–112).

Donald Trump isn't interested in the least in Christianity or the church, except what they can do for him to get elected and strangle democracy. Imagine, if you will for a moment, what our country would be like under another Trump presidency.

His Personal Life Is Abysmal

Boastful and Arrogant

Donald Trump has been heard to say:

> "I am a very smart person."
> "I am a very stable genius."
> "I am the only one to tell you the facts."
> "I know more than anyone on earth."

Lack of Empathy

Trump's delay on responding to the virus cost thousands of lives.

He had no problem separating children from their parents at the southern border.

He fired scores of his cabinet members and other staff.

Sexual Indiscretion Exploiting Women and Promiscuity

He bragged that he had groped (women) and kissed them without their consent. I quote Peter Wehner, a popular commentator on politics and senior fellow at the Ethics and Public Policy Center. He was senior advisor in the George W. Bush White House:

> ". . . Donald Trump—a foul mouthed, non-church attending former Casino owner and reality television star who once endorsed partial-birth abortion [and] was convincingly accused of paying hush money to cover up an affair with a porn star, which took place after his third wife gave birth to their son." (Wehner, Peter, *The Death of Politics*, Harper One, New York, 2019, p.62.)

We already knew that Trump lived a sexual life that was fundamentally contrary to biblical ethics. "Grab them by the p———y," Trump said in a statement listened to by millions (Ibid., p. 79).

You think you have heard the worst about Trump's philandering? How about this one from Michael Wolff's book *Fire and Fury*. "Trump liked to say that one of the things that made life worth living was getting your friends' wives into bed. In pursuing a friend's wife, he would try to persuade the wife that her husband was not what she thought" (Wolff, Michael, *Fire and Fury*, Little, Brown, Great Britain, 2018, p. 23). (Maybe that's why Trump has so few personal friends!)

"Then there were Trump's sexual indiscretions. Divorce was one thing, rumors of sexual escapades another, but the release of *Access Hollywood* tape furnished irrefutable evidence of candidate (Trump) speaking in lewd terms about seducing and assaulting women" (*Jesus and John Wayne* by Kristin Kobes Du Mez, professor of history at Calvin University, a prolific writer whose work appears in *Christianity Today, Christian Century, Washington Post, Religion and Politics,* and other publications).

"To date, Donald Trump has been accused of rape (including his first wife, Ivana, who later dropped the charges), sexual assault, and sexual harassment by more than two dozen women" (Relman, Eliza, "The Twenty-five women who have accused Trump of sexual misconduct," https://www.businessinsider.com/women-accused-trump-sexual-misconduct-list-2017-12. This reference was copied from Sider, Ronald J., Ed., *The Spiritual Danger of Donald Trump*, Cascade Books, Eugene, OR, 2020, p. 26).

"Bragging to Bush, Trump said in the audio, 'I moved in on her, and I failed. I'll admit it. I did try and f——— her. She was married. And I moved in on her very heavily" (Fahrenthold, David A., "Trump recorded having extremely lewd conversation about women in 2005." This reference was copied from Ibid. above.).

Then there is the account of Donald Trump and his illicit relationship with porn star Stormy Daniels (real name, Stephanie Clifford) (Opt. Cit., Sider, p. 141). At present, he is being tried on criminal charges involving this woman.

"Trump has boasted often that he was on the hunt 'almost every night' looking for beautiful young women."

Some of our past presidents have not been paragons of virtue, but they have kept their nefarious activities a secret from their families and the public. When rumors have arisen about events, they have been embarrassed and initially denied their existence. In the case of former president Bill Clinton, he was impeached, acquitted and later resigned his office in disgrace, as president.

In contrast, former president Trump bragged publicly about his immoral behavior with women. A freelance writer Napp Nazworth has written a chapter (4), titled, "Race-Baiter, Misogynist, and Fool." He writes, "The *Access Hollywood* tape showed Trump brag about assaulting women." After the tape was released, ten women came forward and accused Trump of doing what he bragged about doing—groping or kissing them without their consent. "You know, it really doesn't matter what they write as long as you've got a young and beautiful piece of ass. But she's got to be young and beautiful," he said in a 1991 *Esquire* interview (Nazworth, Napp, "Race-Baiter, Misogynist, and Fool," in Sider, Ronald, *The Spiritual Danger of Donald Trump*, Cascade Books, Eugene, OR, 2020, pp. 36–37).

This is an example of the impunity with which former president Trump can carry on his sexual lifestyle. What is most troubling is that his religious supporters explain-away these sordid events. Trump claims to carry on a relationship with God but his behavior doesn't support that (see earlier paragraph on cognitive dissidence).

The following are but a few of many scriptures that address immoral conduct:

Exodus 20:1, 14

Then God spoke all these words saying . . . You shall not commit adultery.

1 Corinthians 6:9–11

Do you not know that the unrighteous will not inherit the kingdom of God? Do not be deceived; neither the sexually immoral nor idolaters nor adulterers . . . will inherit the kingdom of God.

Mark 7:20–23

And he said, "What comes out of a person is what defiles him. For from within, out of the heart of man comes evil thoughts, sexual immorality, theft, murder, adultery, coveting, wickedness, deceit, sensuality, envy . . . All these evil things come from within, and they defile a person."

Matthew 5:27–28

"You have heard that it was said, 'You shall not commit adultery.' But I say unto you that anyone who looks at a woman with lustful intent has already committed adultery with her in his heart."

James 4:4

You adulterous people! Do you not know that friendship with the world is enmity with God. Therefore, whoever wishes to be a friend of the world makes himself an enemy of God.

Rage and Impulsivity

He would throw tantrums and threaten others.

"America is a war zone. He has turned the nation toward anger and violence."

"What I discern, and others, is a pattern of impulsivity that leads to vengeful attacks on those who attack him."

Exaggeration

He would lie about the crowd size at his inauguration.

"I have always gotten more publicity than anybody else."

"He pumped up the immigration crisis at the border to justify the need for building a wall."

He Is a World-Class Liar

He could set a record in *The Guinness World Book of Records* for his number of his lies alone. Peter Wehner, author of *The Death of Politics,* wrote,

> The banality and weaponization of Trump's words are bad enough, but perhaps the greatest cause for concern is his non-stop, dawn to midnight assault on facts, on truth, on reality. (Opt. Cit., Wehner, p. 112)

Manipulation

He enjoys provoking acrimony, malice, and bitterness. This includes turning Americans against each other that they in turn may repeat the manipulation.

He promotes political tribalism

Loyalty to party (or persons) is valued above integrity, truth, and humanity.

Someone has said, "Politics has become the lens through which reality is interpreted, the mold in which attitudes and sensibilities are formed." Peter Wehner addresses this:

> Party loyalty has limits. In this case, the limits were rooted in my belief that Mr. Trump was intellectually, psychologically, and temperamentally unfit to be president. (Ibid., p. 9)

His governance has been unprincipled and often unethical and dishonest

He has had a constant turnover in staff. "In all, 34 percent of the White House Staff was gone in the first year, a number unprecedented in any country not run by pirates" (Wilson, Rick, *Everything Trump Touches Dies,* Free Press, New York, 2019, p. 162).

Rick Wilson is a seasoned political strategist who has published in the *Washington Post, Politico and Rolling Stone.* He has appeared on CNN, MSNBC, and NPR. With his veridical pen, Wilson writes, "Every day that passes gives us additional evidence of how much Trump believes he can govern not under the Constitution and laws of this nation but by fits of pique, fiat, diktat, and by force of will. He doesn't understand or doesn't respect the separation of powers and the structure of government the Founders built" (Ibid., pp. 307–308).

Bob Woodward, associate editor of the *Washington Post,* and well-known author of eighteen books comments in his book *Fear* regarding Trump's dis-use of the advice of others. "Trump rejected the better judgement of almost all of his staff. He had done that before. His perverse independence and irrationality ebbed and flowed" (Opt. Cit., Woodward, p. 252).

"In reality, they (White House staff) spent most of their time fluffing Trump's delicate ego . . . The Trump curse meant this White House was in turmoil the very first day. Unmanaged and unmanageable, this president governs by rage, tweet, and paranoia . . . With a president unable and unprepared for the job and surrounded by a circle of incompetents, toadies, family, reality-TV flotsam, and corporate vassals, the first reset stories hit within days . . . without even the traditional year under their belts, twenty-three White House staffers had been fired or resigned by that point" (Opt. Cit., Wilson, pp. 169–170).

He used fear to capture the support of the people

Trump's campaigns were a carefully plotted and successful effort to exploit the grievances and ire of frightened people who harbored deep suspicions about a political system that was dominated by those who donated huge sums to election campaigns. The fears that Trump exploited included, among others:

- Fear of Islamist terrorist
- Fear of unemployment
- Fear of crime
- Fear of ethnic groups, particularly those at the border
- Fear of environmental crisis

Trump has changed the Republican Party for the worst

The Republican Party transitioned from an organization united by a conservative ideology into an incoherent coalition of conflicting interest bound together by an opposition to a changing America . . . Trump and the Republicans smash norms, break laws, and lie through their teeth with impunity and no consequence . . . The totally normal party was upended when Donald Trump executed a hostile but temporary takeover of the party.

He denied the seriousness of global warming

"I'm not a believer in man-made global warming. It could be warming, and its' going to start to cool down at some point." (www.vox.com/2015/9/22/9368591/trump-global-warming)

He has diminished the seriousness of the COVID-19 pandemic

Trump's denial and slow response cost thousands of American lives and millions of dollars, "in spite of the fact that he had received abundant warnings . . . a tragic failure to proactively mount a focused, whole-of-government and whole-of-society response to indications of a rapidly intensifying public health threat." (www.ncbi.nlm.nih.gov/pmc/articles/PMC9115435)

The following are a few of the dates showing the reluctance of Mr. Trump to act in a timely manner to address the coronavirus facing our country:

- May 2018: The Trump Administration disbands the White House pandemic response team.
- Feb. 10, 2020: "I think the virus is going to be—it's going to be fine."
- Mar. 6, 2020: "You have to be calm. It'll go away."
- Mar. 15, 2020: "Relax"
- Apr. 6, 2020: US death toll passes 10,000.
- Oct. 5, 2020: US death toll passes 210,000. "Don't be afraid of COVID."
- Oct. 10, 2020: "But it's going to disappear; it is disappearing."
- Dec, 31, 2020: US death toll passes 340,000.

Various sources do not agree on the exact number of cases, hospitalizations, and deaths. However, the Centers for Disease Control and Prevention appear to be the most reliable of the (credible sources. Their figures for the US follows: Total Cases: 103,436,829; Hospitalizations: 6,438,882; Deaths: 1,150,119 (reference unavailable).

He doesn't like paying taxes or other bills

"Refusal or delay in paying taxes. Public records show something about Trump and taxes that is deeply troubling. Public records reveal that he is an income tax cheat." Trump promises to build a wall on the Mexican border. "I would build a great wall, and nobody builds better than me, believe me . . . I will have Mexico pay for that wall." (www.politico.com/ story/2015/06/donald-trump-2016-announcment-10-best-lines-119066)

As president (Trump), he did not change his long history of refusing to pay contractors, fighting tax bills, and using two sets of wildly different estimates of the value of his properties.

Sarah Kendzior, author of *Hiding in Plain Sight,* points out in her book that "Trump had not paid federal taxes since 1977 when he became completely tax-exempt in a mysterious agreement between his company and the American government" (Opt. Cit., Kendzior, p. 64.).

Trump and his father, both had a "thing" about not paying taxes and other bills. Jesse Singal, a writer for the "Intelligencer" in *The New York Magazine,* sums it well in the June 9, 2016, issue: "The *USA Today* has posted an explosive investigative story about what appears to a deep aversion GOP nominee Donald Trump has to paying his bills. The short version: *USA Today* claims that, based on what looks like some rather impressive reporting, Trump has for decades looked for any excuse he could find to stiff everyone from plumbers to—can't make this up—lawyers who represented him in non-payment lawsuits."

Mr. Trump has been very cavalier about this "payback" matter. David Cay Johnston, a Pulitzer winner and longtime reporter for the *New York Times,* wrote, "In the spring of 2016, Trump told CNBC: 'I've borrowed knowing that you can pay back with discounts, and I have done very well with debts'" (as well as with lying) (Johnston, David Cay, *The Making of Donald Trump,* Melville House, Brooklyn, 2016, p. 93.).

In another section of David Johnston's book, he writes, "He has been sued thousands of times for refusing to pay employees, vendors, and others. Investors have sued him for fraud in a number of different cities. But among Trump's most highly refined skills is his ability to deflect or shut down law enforcement investigations" (Ibid., xiii).

He wrote, "If people knew more of the truth about Trump and what he is doing to our government, we'd be seeing more protest . . . For example, they have no idea about his years of dealing with a confessed drug dealer, Joseph Weichselbaum . . . Trump covers up crime with scandal . . . In 1991, Trump declared bankruptcy, and by 1992, he had lost all of his signature properties except the Trump Tower . . . No one held Trump accountable" (Opt. Cit., Kendzior, pp.72-76).

Trump Strategies

1. "One of Trump's most successful methods of attack—retaliation: ceaseless insinuations of wrongdoing that provides little or no new information about their target but creates confusion and suspicion"(Ibid. p. 186).

2. Another Trump strategy is "if you say something often enough (true or not), it becomes true." The author also stated explicitly "to get people around him (Trump) to adopt his behavior" (Habberman, Maggie. *Confidence Man,* Penguin Press, New York, 2022, pp. 2, 13.).

3. "He views other people as 'disposable' . . . and people who don't deserve rights, or dignity, or respect" (Opt. Cit., Kendzior, p. 197).

4. "He exploits the common weakness of news reporting—the recitation of 'facts' without analysis of that which goes unsaid" (reference unavailable).

5. "Trump distorts information, contradicts himself, and blocks inquiry into his conduct" (reference unavailable).

6. "Sowing doubt and threatening litigation are not his only strategies to manage his image and puff up his credentials. Trump also accepts awards—many awards—that he gave to himself, with the help of a friend with a criminal past" (reference unavailable).

Preference for Russia

"Folks aren't freaking out about a literal button. They are freaking out about the mental stability of a man who can kill millions without permission from anybody" (Opt. Cit., Woodword, p. 301).

Helsinki, July 2018: "The shock came when Trump stood at a lectern next to Putin and attacked the U.S. Justice Department and the FBI as well as American Intelligence agencies. Trump took Putin's side against the unanimous and well-documented conclusions of American intelligence agencies, that the Russians interfered in the 2016 presidential election . . . Trump supports letting Russia keep Crimea . . . and attacks the North Atlantic Treaty Organization as obsolete" (Johnson, David Cay. *It's Even Worse Than You Think—What the Trump Administration Is Doing to America*, Simon & Schuster, New York, 2018, p. xii).

Damage to Voting and the Electoral Process

Mr. Trump had a unique habit of claiming fraud on elections, which he lost, and refusing to accept any responsibility. This was part of his conspiracy delusions. Few others, until the advent of Mr. Trump, seemed to be concerned about voter fraud. This paranoia was pervasive through his life experiences. In spite of numerous investigations regarding the fraud charges, no evidence of any such nefarious activity was ever discovered.

Voting and the electoral process is part of the foundation of democracy. But let's begin in the beginning.

The Problem Then
Following the Civil War, Congress passed the Fourteenth and Fifteen Amendments for which the South paid little attention. The Fifteenth Amendment guaranteed that the right to vote would not be denied "on account of race, color, or previous condition of servitude." To say that it was not accepted well is a blatant understatement.

The Supreme Court did the cause no favors "when it limited voting protection, intimidation, and fraud were employed by white leaders to reduce voter registration and turnout among African Americans . . . legislation was used to strictly circumscribe the rights of African Americans to vote through poll taxes, literacy test, grandfather clauses, and whites-only primaries" (britannica.com/event/voting-rights-act).

A Solution
After he became president, Lyndon B. Johnson did a political turn-around. As Texas governor and before, he was racist; afterward, he supported equal rights for black minorities. He led Congress to pass the 1965 Voting Rights Act which suspended literacy test and provided for federal approval of proposed changes to voting laws or procedures . . . and directed the attorney general of the US to challenge the use of poll tax for local and state elections (reference unavailable).

The Problem Today
In one word—*Trumpism!*
"What followed on election night was a two-month assault on the vote, in which Trump and his allies exhausted every avenue to overturn

the will of the people—a sustained effort in which he was aided by Republicans and that led to an unthinkable attack on the nation's very capitol . . . He had steadfastly assaulted the pillars of government and its institutions, attacking their credibility, so when the moment came— when it was time for a lie greater than an altered hurricane map . . . yet history had never before seen such a steady methodical, consistent effort by a national figure, and certainly not an incumbent president, to undermine the country's faith in the outcome of free and fairly conducted elections" (Lemire, Jonathan, *The Big Lie,* Flatiron Books, New York, 2022, p. 120).

CNN writer Maya Brown submitted an article on April 12, 2022, titled, "Attacks on voting rights aren't slowing down and black Americans are in the crosshairs, new report finds . . . the authors say partisan politicians in state legislatures around the country have drafted bills and passed laws making it harder for black Americans to vote and they see no signs of the effort slowing down . . . Historic voter turnout in the 2020 election sparked the beginning of one of the most insidious partisan attacks on voting rights in American history, the authors of the report write" (cnn.com/2022/04/12/us/state-of-the-black-america-voting-report/index.html).

The BBC Reality Check Team provided a report, "US election 2020: Fact-checking Trump team's main fraud claims, November 23, 2020." The article discusses the main allegations they are making of fraud and irregularities, and reports the research that disproves the allegations.

Claim 1: "More votes than registered voters."
Research shows: "Election results for Detroit shows that turnout in the city was just under 50 percent."

Claim 2: "Unexpected surges in Democrat votes."
Research shows: "These spikes can easily be accounted for in the timing of the release of large batches for big cities like Milwaukee and Detroit, which are always skewed heavily Democratic."

Claim 3: "Votes flipped from Trump to Biden."
Research shows: "There is no evidence for this, and none has been provided by the president's legal team."

Claim 4: "The voting machines are owned by the Democrats."
Research shows: In a statement, Dominion Voting Systems said it was a nonpartisan US company and has no ownership relationships with the Clintons or with top Democratic politician, Nancy Pelosi . . . Dominion has made contributions to both Republicans and Democrats."

Claim 5: "Thousands of dead people voted."
Research shows: "There is no evidence to support this; however, there have been occasions when this occurred, but evidence suggest this is not a widespread problem" (bbc.com/news/election-us-2020-55016029).

<u>Reform Is Needed</u>
The lifeblood of our democracy is under threat from voter suppression. Other problems are low voter turnout, false claims of election fraud, purging voter rolls, closure of voting places and frequent change of voter venues, poorly trained voter workers, voter registration obstacles/restrictions, and disenfranchisement of former felons.

Considerations for change:

- Early voting is legal in forty-one states plus the District of Columbia.
- Automatic voter registration has been implemented in sixteen states.
- Thirty-six states have electronic voter registration at DMV offices.
- Sixteen states allow sixteen- and seventeen-year-olds to pre-register and then vote when they are eighteen.
- In eight states, former felons have the right to vote.
- Same day voter registration.
- Online voter registration.

- No voter purges.
- National Election Day Holiday.
- End partial gerrymandering with independent commissions.
- Absentee ballots with no excuses needed.
- Reauthorize the civil right Voting Right Act of 1965.

(democracymatters.org/our-issues/why-we-need-reform)

Damage to Race Relations

Much of what was written about voting can be repeated about race relations. The problems of each rather grew up together.

We'll begin with slavery. "Many consider a significant starting point of slavery to be 1619, when the privateer, The White Lion, brought twenty enslaved Africans to the British colony of Jamestown, Virginia . . . Existing estimates establish that Europeans and American slave traders transported nearly 12.5 million African slaves to the Americas . . . Little thought has been given to the fact that this forced migration deprived the African continent of some of its healthiest and ablest men and women" (history.com/topics/black-history/slavery).

In the seventeenth and eighteenth centuries, African slaves worked mainly on the tobacco, rice, and indigo plantations of the southern coast, and later, rice, sugar, and cotton. In the late eighteenth century, following the invention of the cotton gin, the demand for American cotton mushroomed. With this increased demand, came the demand for more slaves to work the land and harvest and process the cotton and other farm products. By 1860, the enslaved population in the US reached nearly 4 million, with more than half living in the cotton-producing states of the south.

The enslaved people began to organize followed by the Abolitionist Movement. The Underground Railroad was born making it possible for thousands to flee the south to freedom in the north. With the approval of Congress, the Missouri Compromise and the Kansas-Nebraska Act increased the tension to free the slaves as many of the norther states had already done. The tension and unhappiness among the Black people increased dramatically leading to physical violence and the John Brown's Raid on Harper's Ferry.

Abraham Lincoln became president in 1861, and he issued the Emancipation Proclamation on September 22, 1862, which announced, "slaves within any state . . . shall be then, thenceforward, and forever free." Civil rights for black people was not yet fully realized. However, with the passage of the Thirteenth, Fourteenth, and Fifteenth Amendments to the Constitution, African Americans were granted citizenship and the right to vote. The battle was still not over as the white community was slow to open the arms of fellowship to these folks of a different color and culture. It would take the persuasive power of government to force the integration forward, and to this date in 2024, it is still incomplete but improving.

The Civil Rights Movement

The Reconstruction Period following the Civil War was a challenging time as the government attempt to abolish slavery and reintegrate the former Confederate States of America into the United States. As mentioned earlier, the three new Amendments to the Constitution helped to codify the abolition spirit. The sentiments expressed in these amendments were put into the language of the people in Abraham Lincoln's Emancipation Proclamation given on January 1, 1863.

The following sub-movements had to be overcome for the progress of Civil Rights to move forward:

(1) Jim Crow Laws.

To marginalize black people and keep them separate from white people, these laws were established in the south beginning in the late nineteenth century. Black people couldn't use the same facilities as white people; live in the same towns together; go to the same schools together; eat in the same facilities together or mix with white people in churches. Interracial marriage was illegal and most blacks could not vote because they were unable to pass voter literacy test.

(2) End of discrimination in the military.

World War II was a turning point in Civil Rights. Initially, black people were not welcome in the military. On June 25, 1941, President Franklin D. Roosevelt issued Executive Order 8802 which opened national defense jobs and other government jobs to all Americans regardless of race, creed, color, or national origin. The Tuskegee Airmen broke the racial barriers to become the first black military aviators earning more than 150 Distinguished Flying Crosses. At the beginning of the Cold War in 1948, President Harry Truman initiated a civil rights agenda by issuing Executive Order 9981 putting an end to discrimination in the military.

(3) Rosa Parks refused to give up her seat on the bus.

On December 1, 1955, a forty-two-year old black woman named Rosa Parks refused to move to the back of the bus when ordered to by the driver. At that time, there was segregation in seating on the buses and black people were required to sit in the back of the bus.

(4) The Little Rock Nine were refused entrance to Central High School.

In 1954, the Supreme Court made segregation illegal in public schools in the case of *Brown v. Board of*

Education. That same year, nine black students, known as *The Little Rock Nine*, arrived at Central High School to begin classes. Governor Faubus had called out the Arkansas National Guard and they were not enrolled. This happened again with similar results. Finally, President Dwight D. Eisenhower intervened and ordered federal troops to escort the Little Rock Nine to and from classes at Central High School.

(5) Civil Rights Act of 1957

On September 9, 1957, President Eisenhower signed the Civil Rights Act into law, which allowed federal prosecution of anyone who tried to prevent someone from voting.

(6) Sit-In at Woolworth's Lunch Counter

On February 1, 1960, four black college students refused to leave a Woolworth's lunch counter without being served. Over the next several days, this practice was observed and joined by others. Some were arrested and charged with trespassing. Protesters launched a boycott of all segregated lunch counters until the owners caved in and the original four students were finally served at the Woolworth's lunch counter where they previously had been turned away.

(7) Freedom Riders

On May 14, 1961, thirteen freedom riders, including black and white protesters, boarded a Greyhound bus in Washington, DC, to tour the American south to test the Supreme Court decision in *Boynton v. Virginia.* This decision declared the segregation of interstate transportation facilities unconstitutional. At different points, mobs mounted the bus and violence followed. One bus was set on fire and the riders were badly beaten. After that, they had police escort for a time. Later, they were arrested and sent to jail. The matter reached the Supreme Court and the charges were reversed. Hundreds of Freedom Riders joined the cause.

(8) March on Washington

One of the most famous events of the Civil Rights Movement took place August 28, 1963. It was organized and attended by several black leaders, including the Reverend Martin Luther King Jr. More than 200,000 people of all races gathered in Washington, DC, for a peaceful march for the purpose of forcing civil rights legislation and establishing job equality for everyone. The height of the march was King's speech, "I Have a Dream," which galvanized the national civil rights movement and became their slogan.

(9) Civil Rights Act of 1964

President John F. Kennedy initiated the legislation and President Lyndon B. Johnson signed the Civil Rights Act of 1964 into law, which guaranteed equal employment for all and limited the use of voter literacy test.

(10) Bloody Sunday

On March 7, 1965, six-hundred peaceful demonstrators participated in the Selma to Montgomery march to protest the killing of black civil rights activist Jimmie Lee Jackson by white police and to encourage legislation to enforce the Fifteenth Amendment. As the group reached the Edmund Pettus Bridge, they were blocked by Alabama State and local police sent by Alabama Governor George C. Wallace. The protesters moved forward and were viciously beaten and teargassed. Dozens of protesters were hospitalized.

(11) Voting Right Act of 1965

When President Lyndon Johnson signed the new Voting Rights Act, he took the Civil Rights Act several steps further. The new law banned all voter literacy tests and provided federal examiners in various voting jurisdictions. As a result, poll taxes were later declared unconstitutional in *Harper v. Virginia State Board of Education* in 1966.

(12) Fair Housing Act of 1968

The Fair Housing Act became law on April 11, 1968. It prevented housing discrimination based on race, sex, national origin and religion.

"The efforts of civil rights activists and countless protesters of all races brought about legislation to end segregation, black voter suppression, and discriminatory employment and housing practices."

Source: The above Civil Rights material was used as written and paraphrased with comments from this author. *Civil Rights Movement* by History.com editors, updated January 22, 2024. history.com/topics/black-history/civil-rights-movement.

The Cognitive Dissonance of Donald Trump about minorities
The former president has repeatedly proclaimed that he "was the least racist person in the US." In his distorted mind, he probably believes that. His behavior and language belie the truth of his statement, hence, his *cognitive dissonance.* To support the claim of Donald Trump's racism,

all one must do is to look at "Donald Trump's long history of racism, from the 1970s to 2020," as documented by German Lopez, a Vox reporter on August 13, 2020. Lopez comments, "Trump has repeatedly claimed he's 'the least racist person that you've ever encountered' ". His history suggests otherwise prior to his presidency. See summary from Lopez's article below:

- **1973:** The US Department sued the Trump Management Corporation for violating the Fair Housing Act.
- **1992:** The Trump Plaza Hotel had to pay a $200,000 fine because it transferred black and women dealers off tables to accommodate a big-time gambler's prejudices.
- **2000:** When the St. Regis Mohawk Tribe proposed a casino, Trump saw that as a threat to his casinos in Atlanta City, and ran a series of ads suggesting that the tribe had a "record of criminal activity [that] is well documented."
- **2011:** Trump played a big role in pushing the rumor that president Obama was not born in the US and, thus, unable to qualify to be president.

His history suggests continuing racism after he became a candidate and president

- **2015:** Trump launched his campaign by calling Mexican immigrants rapists who are bringing crime and bringing drugs to the US. He promised to build a wall to keep them out.
- **2016:** In a pitch to black voters, Trump said, "You're living in poverty, your schools are no good, you have no jobs and 58 percent of your youth are unemployed."
- **2017:** Trump reportedly said that people who come to the US from Haiti, "all have AIDS", and the people who come from Nigeria would never "go back to their huts" once they saw America.
- Trump later tweeted that several black and brown members of Congress "are from countries whose governments are a

complete and total catastrophe" and they should "go back" to those countries.
(vox.com/2016/7/25/12270880/donald/-trump-racist-racism-history)

Sued for Discrimination
"The Housing Section of the federal Justice Department served notice to Trump Management, Inc., they were being sued for discriminatory rental practices against black tenants . . . This was not an accident. Prospective black tenants told authorities stories about being blocked by a building superintendent or being denied the same apartment repeatedly" (Opt. Cit., Haberman, p. 31.).

Trump's Leadership toward Secularism or the Normalization of Evil

Donald Trump's immoral behavior has flowered in a permissive and amoral culture. This partially explains why the religious community has been slow and reluctant to condemn his immoral behavior. This in no way excuses his bad behavior but does help to explain the growing trend to secularize our culture that was formerly painted with the Judeo-Christian brush.

To illustrate our growing drift toward secularism, I want to use the Southern Baptist Convention as an example. I can speak objectively about this religious group as I was reared in it from my birth. I was immersed weekly in Bible study, catechism, church attendance and all the accoutrements of conservativism and fundamentalism. I was baptized at age seven, ordained to the ministry at age seventeen, and educated in a Southern Baptist University and seminary. I pastored Southern Baptist Churches for nine years serving in various offices and denominational committees. I performed numerous weddings and funerals and occasionally led revival meetings. I organized the church and associational structures and trained many for leadership roles.

I witnessed subtle changes in the religious environment and a decline in spirituality. In the early 1980s, my beloved denomination was taken over by a small group of fundamentalists who purged the leadership on several levels dismissing moderate trustees and employees. This was followed by an exodus of seventeen hundred Southern Baptist Churches who formed two additional conventions. I left Southern Baptists but maintained my Baptist Heritage, and moved into the field of Christian Social Ministry.

This cultural shift brought with it a decline in civility and human decency and a dramatic slide in church membership and attendance. Years later, Mr. Trump would capitalize on the despondency and confusion left by the erosion of values and morality over time.

Despite its losses, the Southern Baptist Convention was still the largest Protestant denomination in the United States numbering fourteen million members in forty-seven thousand churches. Fundamentalism had weakened the moral fabric and principled practices of the once great denomination. Among other deficits, a discovery was made about "how leaders at the highest levels of the Southern Baptist Convention dealt with sex abuse claims over the course of more than twenty-five years . . . It showed a depth of callousness, defense of immoral behavior, and depravity that rivals that of the Catholic Church's scandals of twenty years ago" (theledger.com/story/opinion/2022/05/31/shocking-report-reveals-depth-hypocricy-southern-baptist-leaders/9924240002/).

What happened to Southern Baptists was a small sample of what was going on in other denominations and the culture at large. A report from the Barna Research group described this in detail:

> Christian morality is being ushered out of American social structures and off the cultural main stage, leaving a vacuum in its place—and the broader culture is attempting to fill the void. New research from Barna reveals growing concern about the moral

condition of the nation, even as many American adults admit they are uncertain about how to determine right from wrong . . . Is truth relative or absolute? And do Christians see truth and morality in radically different ways from the broader public, or are they equally influenced by the growing tide of secularism and religious skepticism?" (barna.com/research/the-end-of-absolutes-Americas-new-moral-code/)

Democracy is also part of the sweep that is being flushed away as the old is making way for the new. This "new morality" explains a great deal about the impunity Donald Trump is experiencing in his immoral behavior. This "new morality" is desensitizing the culture, including government and religion, allowing for an overhaul of society's moral conscience.

Sadly, we've come a long way since married couples had to sleep in separate beds on movie screens and curse words were stricken from movie scripts. Certainly, lewd dress was *verboten.*

Ronald Sider in his chapter in the book he edited *The Spiritual Danger of Donald Trump* states that Donald Trump "reveals in his books the fact that he gets to sleep with some of the top women of the world" (Sider, Ronald, *The Spiritual Danger of Donald Trump,* Cascade Books, Eugene, OR, 2020, p. 89).

The fact that the American people would accept a man like that, with the added baggage of chronic liar, deceiver, divider, vote-stealer, encourager of violence, and leadership of a mob to attack the US Capitol is a sad commentary on the present American character.

One more thing. "If a novelist had concocted a villain like Trump—a larger-than-life, over-the-top avatar of narcissism, demagoguery, and tyrannical impulses . . . She or he would likely be accused of extreme contrivance and implausibility" (Opt. Cit. Kakutaini. pp. 15–16).

"Trump has worked hard to make sure few people know about his lifelong entanglement with a major cocaine trafficker, with mobsters, con artists and swindlers. He has been sued thousands of times for refusing to pay employees, vendors, and others. Investors have sued him for fraud in a number of different cities. But among Trump's most highly refined skills is his ability to deflect or shut down law enforcement investigations. He uses threats of litigation" (*The Making of Donald Trump* by David Cay Johnson, Pulitzer Prize winner, long-time reporter for *The New York Times*. Opt. Cit., Johnston—Making of D.T.—p. xiii).

Our democracy will slip further into an autocracy in which he will ultimately control the government and the social institutions.

His cabinet and staff will be minions who always agree with him and never go against his wishes.

He will pardon all of his own crimes and reorganize the Justice Department and the federal court system further affirming his own agenda.

His chronic lying and deceit will lay the foundation for a reality that follows his own degenerate thinking.

In time, I believe he will create a Department of Indoctrination (education?) that will shape the curriculum our children are taught.

He will continue to disenfranchise our trade agreements with other nations and participate in relationships that only he can control.

He will manage to control elections resulting in a perpetual, non-ending term of office.

I can't even imagine what will be the fate of the chronically ill, the poor, the disabled, and the aged.

The Mental Health of Donald Trump

A very limited number of writers who take on Donald Trump's story talk about his mental health. They do describe in detail the symptoms of maladjustment, involving his language and behavior. They describe his violence, narcissism, lying, deceit, and the danger he is to democracy and the entire world. The one exception is a book edited by Dr. Brandy Lee, MD, M. Div. She was Assistant Clinical Professor in Law and Psychiatry at Yale School of Medicine and teaches at Yale Law School. She leads a Violence Prevention Alliance collaborators project for the World Health Organization and is the author of over one hundred peer-reviewed articles, editor of eleven academic books, and author of the book *Violence*.

For purposes of this book, we will discuss in some detail a book she edited titled *The Dangerous Case of Donald Trump* and who writes some of the chapters in the book. This book is a collection of essays written by thirty-seven psychiatrists and other mental health professionals. It describes in detail various psychopathologies that these professionals see in the behavior and language of the former president (Lee, Brandy, *The Dangerous Case of Donald Trump*, St. Martin's Press, New York, 2017.).

Trump's ridiculousness, his narcissistic ability to make everything about himself, the outrageousness of his lies, and the profundity of his ignorance can easily distract attention from the more lasting implications of his story.

"Trumpism is more a political playbook than anything else:

- Sowing racial division to turn out the base is acceptable.
- Lying is not only okay, it's encouraged.
- The press is the enemy of the people.
- The will of the people is at best an annoying speed bump on the path to maintaining power.
- Propaganda is the preferred method of communication.

- Winning at all costs is okay no matter the morals, laws, or consequences to the country" (Pfeiffer, Dan. *Un-Trumping America,* Twelve, New York, 2020, p. 5).

"It doesn't take a psychiatrist to notice that our president (Trump) is mentally compromised" (Opt. Cit., Lee, p. 7).

Among the many disturbing behaviors of this man now serving as the leader of the free world, is his relationship to his daughter, Ivanka . . . "I've said if Ivanka wasn't my daughter, perhaps I'd be dating her," in "A Clinical Case for the Dangerousness of Donald J. Trump," article by Dr. Diane Jhueck. This writer was in private practice for several decades and performed numerous mental health evaluations on individuals who represented a threat to themselves or others. She also founded several charity organizations (Opt. Cit., Lee, p. 186.).

"I would come to understand that questions of right and wrong didn't matter to Trump in the slightest—all that counted to him, and then to me, was winning and displaying blind loyalty". This was revealed in Michael Cohen's book, Disloyal. Cohen was personal lawyer, fixer, and Special Counsel to President Donald Trump from 2017 and 2018, and Executive Vice-President for the Trump Organization (Cohen, Michael, *Disloyal,* Skyhouse, New York, 2020, p. 32.).

Unethical Business Practices

Because of the high position that Mr. Trump holds, he can arrange for income producing conferences to be held in his luxurious hospitality faculties where attendees pay exorbitantly high overnight fees to attend the conference. That is much less than copacetic when it comes to ethical business practice, but it doesn't seem to bother Mr. Trump in the least.

Next in order of unscrupulousness would be that of Trump's chilling habit of refusing to pay his contractors or find a way to avoid paying taxes. And the icing on the money cake is his inflation of the value of his properties. If it's not too late to add one more prick in this prickly pear, Trump prefers not to add his signature to his routine financial statements. And he gets away with it! Rich Wilson writes with his acidic pen a good summary for this section:

> "He used his position as president as a marketing tool for his hotels and country clubs in Mar-a-Lago, Bedminister, and Doral, Florida. He's made his downtown DC hotel a go-to place for foreign and domestic lobbyists to rent suites of rooms at ludicrously jacket-up prices and to rent ballrooms for events." He follows up with, "It's not that it's just corrupt; it's shabby and low corruption" (Opt. Cit., Wilson, p. 176.).

CHAPTER 4

THE LOSS AND DAMAGE TRUMP HAS CAUSED THE COUNTRY AND DEMOCRACY

The Damage Begins with Losses

This chapter is about the loss we have experienced in our country in recent years and the resulting damage that has followed. As earlier expressed in careful detail, much of the blame for recent losses involve our past president Donald Trump. We will review some of those losses, but our nation is no stranger to loss.

Many citizens have believed that institutions have failed them and they are fed the crumbs that the "elite" have given them. Our nation is divided between the "haves" and the "have-nots," and the "have-nots" have become angry and have threatened to make changes. As an example, we have witnessed the tragic and deadly storming of the capitol and unfortunately, there are those who believe that, or something worse, will happen again—you can count on it.

Very few of our citizens would not admit that changes are in order, even though our Constitution and Bill of Rights allow recourse for injustices.

We have suffered serious problems before, but part of the present crisis is different in that we previously have had men and women of integrity and courage that have inspired our citizenry to be at their very best and set the example for character and courage, and who listened to their better angels.

We complain and moan, "Ain't it awful," and Pogo, a comic character, has best captured the spirit of the cause of our problems when he said, "We have met the enemy, and he is us." In other words, we have shot ourselves in the foot, which has demonstrated our lack of courage and obedience to the principles that have made our nation the shining light, long valued in the world. (That light is flickering.) I hope this book will challenge readers to examine their own aspirations and desires and be a part of a mighty new wave of patriotism and faith that will wash away the moral filth, cynicism, and hopelessness that has polluted our nation in recent years.

A Changing America

I repeat myself, but it must be emphasized that our national problems did not begin with our former president, although he has taken advantage of the angry and apathetic mood that hovers over our disenchanted countrymen. And while we are making new promises about what we are going to do, let us not forget to kick ourselves on our backside for not being more alert, courageous, and for putting up with his nonsense and unbelievably poor behavior and disgusting lack of good presidential management.

So many writers have described the uniqueness and seriousness of these times when our very democracy is threatened. One example is that of Andrew Prokop of Vox Media, who has written,

> American Democracy is in grave peril. It is besieged on all sides, the threats culminating so far in Donald Trump's attempt to steal the 2020 presidential election

from Joe Biden . . . dark scenarios for the future have been posed . . . One of the threats is that of stolen elections and voter suppression. I would add two others; fear and intimidation. (Prokop, Andrew. *VOX*, "American Democracy is Under Threat. But What is That Threat Exactly?" January 25, 2022. Vox.com/22798975/democracy-threats-peril-trump-voting-rights.)

Our nation, "The City on a Hill," lost its innocence following a bitter Civil War, two bloody world wars and a series of regional conflicts. The nonmilitary causalities of war far outnumber the battlefield injuries and deaths. The assault on the family was overwhelming, involving lengthy separations, divorce, children raised without one parent, blended families, increase in alcoholism, drug abuse, mental illness, and increase in juvenile delinquency.

America was changing in many ways. Some were positive and many were not. As men went off to war, a personnel vacuum was left in businesses and industry which the women filled, learning new skills that would remain with many of them for the rest of their lives. In addition, the seeds were planted for the feminist movement and women's rights. The dark side of this was that many children were left unsupervised at home diminishing their preparation for mature development and not having a model for normal family life. The code for sexual morality was forever changed and became part of a new culture dominated by fear, selfishness, pleasure, and egocentrism.

This disruption in values and principles impacted education, religion, politics, and economics. However, there were movements that arose to preserve the past and resist any new changes. There was a desire to keep or bring back an era which was a more comfortable, dependable, less complex, and a more peaceful time. That was a time of security, certainty, and integrity. With industrialism, modernism, and globalization entering the American culture, many would resist and fight this new modern movement. The losses were beginning to add up.

Our politics shifted to the left and our traditional moral and religious values took a dramatic change. Taxes increased and church attendance decreased. Increased mobility, communications and globalization were enablers of this rapidly changing world. The Supreme Court ruled against the long-held practice of allowing prayer and Bible reading in public schools because of a very narrow interpretation of the First Amendment.

The Scopes Trial, formally known as *The State of Tennessee v. John Thomas Scopes* in 1925, came about as a result of a high school teacher being accused of teaching evolution. This was in violation of Tennessee's Butler Act, which made it unlawful to teach this subject in public schools. This continued a growing conservatism in religion and education that only "approved" ideas and theories should be taught in public school curriculum. It is unfortunate that John Dewey's strong belief in applying the scientific method to education did not include the goal of teaching children to think for themselves. This would expose students to various theories which encouraged thinking and making choices based upon their conclusions. The importance of learning to think for one's self should be a primary goal of education.

John Scopes lost the case and was fined, but the case was later overturned. The trial drew national attention and galvanized the fundamentalists who claimed that evolution was contrary to biblical teachings.

All this took place during the early and middle twentieth century, along with the depression and the shift in population from the rural areas to the cities and factory life. The rural folks brought with them to the cities their religious fundamentalism, less formal education, and racial bias along with more positive qualities and skills. Cultural assimilation was slow to take hold and left many holes in the fabric of unity. As agriculture technology improved, most of the farmers were able to adjust to new technology and equipment. However, when it came to their religion and politics, many could not accept new discoveries that brought enhanced understanding to the scriptures and civility to politics. They could not give up what they thought to be the "fundamentals" of the faith. The fundamentalist folks would not accept this new "liberalism" while gladly accepting other progressive changes. The depression, wars, and social upheaval required damage control that began to involve government more and more in solving social problems.

The American far-right began to grow and the government stepped in to solve many of the social and economic problems. First, there was the New Deal, followed by the Great Society, the War on Poverty, Civil Rights, Women's Rights, and Gay Rights. This led to feelings of disenfranchisement in various groups who wanted to stop the spread of liberalism and loss of white supremacy. The fear was real and spread to many areas of the culture. In spite of laws to eliminate racism and other forms of bigotry, there were groups that were disenchanted, believing that conservative control of religious liberty and white dominance were being lost.

In addition to the rise of fundamentalism, America was fighting unpopular conflicts in Korea and Viet Nam in the 1950s through 1975. Violent protest expressed the growing dissatisfaction with the decisions of government creating further feelings of alienation and hate. The following will summarize the making of this fertile soil upon which Trumpism was planted creating the losses we have experienced.

The Loss of Truth

The insidious nature of this change is its incremental, creeping advance. I'm old enough to remember when all stores, except those offering essential services, were closed on Sunday to observe the biblical mandate to not work, but attend worship services— "the Lord blessed the Sabbath day and hallowed it" (Exodus 20:11). Old-timers like me can remember when school classes opened the day by reading the Bible and sometimes praying. Those of us who attended church summer camps remember that the boys and girls had separate swimming times. I also remember that in movies, couples who slept in bed were married and sleep separately in twin beds.

I remember when pregnancy before marriage was a disgrace. In the late 1950s and early 1960s, a gradual change took place. There was more openness about unmarried parenthood and the maternity home population began a decline as the girls chose to remain in their own home. By the mid-1950s, most maternity homes had closed or converted to a different social service.

A permissiveness continued to invade our society that had begun after WWII. This may have arisen due to the tension of war, sacristy, and the discipline for survival. We could "let our hair down" a little now and relax. We and our allies had won the war and we deserved some respite. For example, strictly obeying the letter of the law became honoring the spirit of the law, and such reasoning or rationalization was applied to many disciplines.

Our beloved country was losing its innocence!

I'm sure you get the picture. Many changes were progressive, but some were not. There were signs of confusion as to the changing standards and this ambivalence created uncertainty and even rebellion on the part of the youth in that generation. Orphanages were retooled for group homes and treatment centers for troubled youth. Foster care and adoption became the choice for out-of-home care placements. I was a part of this transformation and developed training programs for parents wanting to provide foster care or adoption. These were good changes and resulted in support for families and permanency for children. The family had been fractured and healing was in order, but not all the wounds could be healed.

The social changes were received in different ways. Many would have the resilience to assimilate the changes or struggle against them. The "strugglers" became bitter and unhappy people. Some would attempt to cope through addiction, mental illness, or criminal behavior. Some simply became angry and antagonistic and lived lives of "quiet desperation" and emptiness.

Many blamed the social institution, religion, and government, and after blaming them for their sad conditions, sought a "savior" that would deliver them from their miserableness.

"When Donald Trump descended the golden escalator to announce his run for president, none of the skeptical media below could have imagined he would win." Roland Hughes and Joshua Nevett, BBC News, June 15, 2019, wrote, "The Day Trump ran for president (and what people predicted)" (bbc.com/news/world-us-canada-48595411).

Donald Trump took advantage of the nation's depressed mood, and promised, "To Make America Great." And much of America loved him. The reasons for this devotion are many and complex, and scholars and pundits alike offer their explanation for this weird and almost macabre new American experience. One writer compares the similarities of Trump with Hitler's motive in seeking power—"A desire to rediscover past greatness, a fear of social disorder, and the longing for a strong leader (Reicher, Stephen D., and Haslam, S. Alexander. "Trump's Appeal: What Psychology Tells Us," *Scientific American,* March 1, 2017. https://www.scientificamerican.com/article/ trump-rsquo-s-appeal-what- psychology-tells-u).

Another writer posits an unusual but very believable explanation. "The glib way to answer the question of his popularity is that a certain percentage of the American public love bigoted demagogues, and that's that." Adding to that, he said, "America has been in love with outlaws since its early days, and leaders like Trump who seem to achieve power while flouting the rules of decorum, exert a kind of magnetic pull" (Ryan, Shane, "Why Is Donald Trump So Appealing to So Many People?" pastemagazine. com/politics/donald-trump-so-appealing-to-so-many-people).

Our country was losing its security.

The above writer offers another reason for Trump's hold on certain groups. "But on a gut level Trump also scares them. And that power of inspiring fear is transmitted to his supporters, because the ability to scare another person, to control them in that way, has been appealing to human beings forever."

Perhaps the view that is most often offered and involves the most people is that he fills a need that has that has been years in the making. He fills an emptiness of being left behind and marginalized in the economy, and disappointed with government leadership. People said of Mr. Trump, "He is one of us, and has promised to fix everything that has gone wrong. He picked up on this, as he is a good reader of crowds, and coined a motto, 'I can fix it . . . Nobody can fix it like I can" (en. wikipedial.org/wiki/i_alone_can_fix_it).

This book is about the loss America has experienced under the leadership of former president Donald Trump. I want us to understand loss, as it is used in this book, embraces more than the removal of something that is never returned. It also includes damage, which is closely related. For example, I may have an expensive watch, which has been damaged to the extent that its function to keep time may be lost. Closer to the theme of this book, another example. I may have an employee who is badly hurt in an accident. He is alive and is still on my payroll, but his service to me is temporarily lost.

In my research for this book, I have read several authors who describe the losses that America and democracy has experienced as a result of our former president's decisions and behavior. It would be more accurate to describe the damage he has done, resulting in the loss of intangible matters rather that the loss of our nation or democracy. However, if the damage is not repaired, our democracy and freedom CAN be lost.

Our basic values of truth, integrity, and selflessness are gradually being compromised and even diminished. Mr. Trump's narcissism and self-centeredness has blinded him to higher values and robbed him of the satisfaction and joy of reaching out to others and have others to value him. Values guide behavior and provide a benchmark for measuring improvement. High values are prized and open many doors of opportunity, as well as generating respect. Truth and reality give structure to our lives and stability to our mental status.

Glenn Kessler is the editor and chief writer of the *Washington Post* Fact Checker team. He has written the introduction to the book published by the newspaper containing the report on Donald Trump's lies. The following are excerpts from the book:

> From the start of Trump's presidency, *The Washington Post* Fact Checker Team catalogued every false or misleading statement he has made. As of January 20, 2020, three years after Trump took the oath of office, the count stood at 16,241 . . . But the pace of deception has quickened exponentially . . . Some days are simply astonishing: on September 7, 2018, he made 125 claims. On December 18, 2019, 126 claims; on November 5, 2018, 139 claims; etc. This book is not simply a catalogue of false claims; it is a guide to Trump's attack on the truth . . . In the age of Trump, there is evidence that Republicans have grown less concerned about presidents being honest than they were a decade ago." (Opt. Cit., Kessler, pp. x, xi, xii, xiii.)

Dr. Gail Sheehy, PhD, has written an article in *The Dangerous Case of Donald Trump* edited by Dr. Brandy Lee, MD. The article's author is an author, journalist, and popular lecturer. She has written seventeen books including her revolutionary, *Passages,* named as one of the most influential books of our times. In her article, "Trump's Trust Deficit Is the Core Problem," she writes, "To the dismay of even conservative observers, Trump appears totally indifferent to the truth . . . Trump creates his own extreme manipulation of reality" (Opt. Cit., Lee, p. 81.).

Along with other sad matters, the act of lying is picked up by his staff. His staff counselor, Kellyanne Conway chose to use the term "alternative facts" to label his lies. Rudy Giuliani, another staff member, said "Truth isn't truth, explaining that everyone has their own version of truth" (Opt. Cit., Kessler, p. 261).

The worldwide millions of Christians and Jews follow the Judeo-Christian tradition, which teachings are described in the Holy Bible and have become the moral foundation of western civilization. Other religions have their holy books, which guide their way of living. Both the Old and New Testaments in the Bible are seriously clear about the evil of lying and deceit beginning with the Ten Commandments recorded in Exodus 20:16.

> "You shall not give false testimony against your neighbor."

The following scriptures are a small sample of verses directing believers to be truthful. This is an important "stone" in the foundation of civilization.

> Do not lie. Do not deceive one another.
> —Leviticus 19:11 NIV

> Truthful lips endure forever . . . a false witness will not go unpunished and he who pours out lies will parish.
> —Proverbs 12:19; 19:9 NIV

> A false witness will not go unpunished, and he who pours out lies will not go free.
> —Proverbs 19:5 NIV

Therefore, each of you must put off falsehood and speak truthfully.

—Ephesians 4:25 NIV

You belong to your father, the devil . . . for there is no truth in him. When he lies, he speaks his native language, for he is a liar and the father of lies.

—John 8:44 NIV

Whoever would love life and see good days must keep his tongue from evil and his lips from deceitful speech.

—1 Peter 3:10 NIV

It is sad that some of most popular Christian leaders, solidly with exceptions, are behind Mr. Trump. What is surprising and disturbing is that many in Christian leadership have almost given him *Messianic* qualities. Here are just a few of those leaders.

Ralph Reed, former head of the Christian Coalition and Founder and Chairman of the Faith and Freedom Coalition, stated, "evangelicals have a moral obligation to enthusiastically back Trump in the upcoming election (https://www.newsmax.com/newsfront/evangelicals-christians-ralph-reed-trump/2019/10/09/id/936344).

Franklin Graham, President and CEO of Samaritan's Purse and the Billy Graham Evangelistic Association, said, "There is almost a 'demonic power' at work in opposition to Trump."

Jerry Falwell Jr., President of Liberty University, who later resigned following discovery that he and his wife were involved in a sexual scandal.

Jack Graham, Senior Pastor of Prestonwood Baptist Church in Dallas, who wrote an op-ed letter in the *Christian Post*, "Why it is Wise for Christians to Support President Trump?"

Robert Jeffress, Senior Pastor of First Baptist Church in Dallas, Texas, Trump's most enthusiastic evangelical supporters. "Sadly, he has unapologetically called Christians who oppose Trump, 'spineless morons,' Immoral, Demonic, Prideful, Blind, Stupid, and Lacking in Grace (Opt. Cit., Sider, p. 134.).

Mark DeMoss, a former chief of staff to Moral Majority founder, Jerry Falwell Sr., asked the question to author, Sarah Posner, that has been on the minds of many of us:

> How do people who have spent their entire adult life preaching religious piety, moral purity, and so-called family values, just flip a switch and endorse a candidate who doesn't reflect what they have been preaching and telling congregations what they should be looking for. How do people who their whole lives live by Jesus's way, suddenly make an about face?" (Posner, Sarah. *Unholy*, Random House, New York, 2020, Pages 12.)

Many attempts have been made to understand the cognitive dissonance of Christians supporting a man so corrupt and immoral. Authors express this enigma in their essay, "Setting Your Own Rules and Cognitive Dissonance," in the book Ronald Sider edited:

> "A paradox of the Trump presidency is that the most irreligious presidency in at least one hundred years is being hailed in messianic language by conservative evangelical Christians who remain loyal despite prosecutions, corruption, and impeachment . . . Too many conservative Christians make a habit of rejecting verifiable truth by giving priority to a sort of blind faith that justifies the cognitive dissonance they experience . . . A Baylor religious group conducted in 2017 (reference no longer available) by a team of

sociologists discovered that Christian nationalism was
the foundation of Trump's religious support.

Mark Galli, in his article, "Why 'Mere' Words Matter," he tries to
explain this paradox:

> "As I've argued, it is deeply troubling that Mr. Trump's
> evangelical supporters refuse to condemn the president's
> unethical behavior in office. That failure stands in
> sharp contrast to their reaction to Bill Clinton's moral
> failings . . . (reflected) in a 1998 Southern Baptist
> resolution. "We implore our government leaders to live
> by the highest standards of morality both in their private
> actions and in their public duties . . . and thereby serve
> as models of moral excellence and character." (Galli,
> Mark, "Why 'Mere' Words Matter, Opt. Cit., Sider,
> pp. 7–8.)

I hope this doesn't reflect a growing tolerance for immoral behavior in
public leaders as purported by the news, media, theater, and motion
pictures. Moral relativism has been growing for years,

A closing thought on this subject: "No one will take Christianity
seriously if we shout about the moral injustices of past presidents but
are struck dumb when it comes to the (greater) moral injustices of the
current (Ibid., Trump, p. 29.).

Closely related to the loss of values is the loss of integrity, civility, and respect

That is a loss we can ill afford. It is a part of America's character and
foundation of democracy. Our former president is too absorbed in
himself to care about the feelings or value of others. So many of our
nation's problems stem from lack of respect and the desire to have one's

own way. Our politics is crippled and nonproductive because our leaders have forgotten how to agree to disagree.

Ileana Ros-Lehtinen, a senior advisor at Akin Gump and who represented South Florida in the legislature for three decades, wrote the following: "Now we think we must fight to the death, to cling stubbornly to our positions and cede no ground. On all sides of the political spectrum, we stick to our own views because to do otherwise would seem weak (and perhaps disloyal to their party). It is not enough that I win. I must insist that you lose" (Ros-Lehtinen, Ileana, "We have forgotten what respect is." *Politico Magazine,* "What Trump Showed Us About America," 11/19/2020. Politico.com/news/magazine/2020/11/19/roundup-what-trump-showed-us-about-america-435762).

Michiko Kakutani, a Pulitzer Prize winning literary critic, earlier mentioned, wrote in one of her books, *The Death of Truth* about the growing nihilism in Washington, saying "it is both an echo and a cause of more widespread feelings; a reflection of a growing loss of faith in institutions and a loss of respect for both the rule of law and everyday norms and traditions; a symptom of our loss of civility, our growing inability to have respectful debates with people who have opinions different from our own; our growing unwillingness to give others the benefit of the doubt . . . the courtesy of a hearing." Civility is almost a lost art. Civility is just not in the repertoire of Trump's dealing with people (Opt. Cit., Kakutani, p. 155.).

Dr. Mary Trump, in her book about her uncle, wrote, "The simple fact is that Donald is fundamentally incapable of acknowledging the suffering of others" (Opt. Cit., Trump, p. 210.).

The apostle Paul addressed poor interpersonal relationship in the church at Philippi when he wrote his letter to them recorded in the New Testament:

Finally brothers, whatever is true, whatever is noble, whatever is right, whatever is pure, whatever is lovely, whatever is admirable—if anything is excellent or praiseworthy—think about such things. (Philippians 4:8 NIV)

Not bad advice for all of us.

The Damage to Reality

This section is so very important. In my research, I came across a statement that made the hair on my arm stand up. I could hardly believe what I was reading. Peter Wehner, who covers American politics and conservative thought and worked for the Bush, Carter, and Regan Administration, describes these frightening comments by Scottie Nell Hughes on the *Diane Rehn Show*: "Everybody has a way of interpreting (facts) to be true, or not true. There is no such thing, unfortunately, anymore as facts . . . truth isn't truth . . . (truth is) merely subjective, utterly pliable, and completely in the eye of the beholder" (Opt. Cit., Wehner, p. 122).

This chapter described the opinion of several journalists, psychiatrists, military personnel, and other professionals who had varying degrees of contact with the former president. This section will list the aberrant thoughts and behavior that many of them described in unflattering terms.

The former president has had a problem with lying for most of his life. The Fact Checker Staff of *The Washington Post* monitored his (Trump) State of the Union speeches, campaign rallies, and major speeches from the time he took office until January 20, 2020. During this three-year time period, the false and misleading statements numbered 16,241. The authors adds,

> And then there is Donald Trump, the most mendacious president in US history. He almost never expresses regret. He's not known for one big lie—just a constant

stream of exaggerated, invented, boastful, purposely outrageous, spiteful, inconsistent, dubious, and false claims . . . From the start of Trump's presidency, *The Washington Post* Fact Checker team has catalogued every false or misleading statements he has made. As of January 20, 2020, three years after Trump took the oath of office, the count stood at 16,241. (Washington Post Fact-checker Staff. *Donald Trump and the Assault on Truth,* Scribner, New York, p. x)

In the same book, the authors respond to his claim that Mr. Trump received only a $1 million loan from his father to get his start.

After examining more than 100,000 confidential documents, the *New York Times* concluded that Fred's 'small loan' was actually $60.7 million or $140 million dollars in 2018 dollars, much which was never repaid . . . In all, the *Times* found Trump received the equivalent of at least $41.3 million in today's dollars from his father's real estate empire. (Ibid., p.34.)

Dr. Robert Lifton has written over twenty books and taught at Yale and Harvard Universities as well as the City University of New York. In one of his last books, *Losing Reality: On Cults and the Mindset of Political and Religious Zealotry,* he writes the following:

David Leonhardt, the journalist who has probably done the most to track Trump' lies, describes him (with cowriters) as "virtually indifferent to reality, often saying whatever helps him make the case he's trying to make" and as "trying to make truth irrelevant." It is difficult to overestimate the dangers that stem from such extreme assaults on reality by a man who holds the most powerful office in the world . . . I have found that the mind can simultaneously believe and not believe in

> something and can move in and out of belief according
> to personal pressures. (Lifton, Robert Jay. *Losing Reality*,
> The New Press, 2019, 159)

Sarah Posner, earlier mentioned, is a reporting fellow with Type Investigations and her coverage and analysis of politics and religion has appeared in *The New York Times, The Washington Post, Politico,* and other venues. In her book, *Unholy,* chapter 10, "The Assault on Reality," she writes, "No previous Republican candidate or president has embraced, perpetuated, and enabled such a staggering exhibition of lies and conspiracy theories and used his bully pulpit to degrade his perceived enemies" (Opt. Cit., Posner, p. 257).

Tony Schwartz is an American journalist who specializes in books about business. He is best known for ghostwriting former president Donald Trump's book, *Trump: The Art of the Deal.* For twenty-five years, he has contributed articles and served in book company management for *The New York Post, Newsweek, The New York Times, The New York Magazine, and Esquire.* Of all the books, he has had some part in publishing, he has stated that he regrets his involvement with Trump's book, *The Art of the Deal.*

In Dr. Brandy X. Lee's book, *The Dangerous Case of Donald Trump,* with contributions from twenty-seven psychiatrists and other mental health experts, Tony Schwartz writes a chapter titled "I Wrote the Art of the Deal with Donald Trump" with the byline "His Self-Sabotage is Rooted in His Past." The following are excerpts from this chapter:

> "Many of the deals in *The Art of the Deal* were massive
> failures—among them the casinos he owned and
> the launch of a league to rival the National Football
> League—but Trump had me to describe each of them
> as a huge success" (Schwart, Tony. "I Wrote the *Art of
> the Deal* With Donald Trump," in Lee, Brandy, *The*

Dangerous Case of Donald Trump, St. Martin's Press, New York, 2017, pp. 70–71.).

"What's clear is that he has spent his life seeking to dominate others, whatever that requires and whatever collateral damage it creates along the way" (Ibid., p. 71).

"The capacity to delay gratification, or, above all, a conscience, an inner sense of right and wrong. Trump simply did not traffic in emotions or interest in others" (Ibid., p. 71).

"A key part of that story is that facts are whatever Trump deems them to be" (Ibid. 71).

Michael D'Antonio is a Pulitzer Prize journalist who has authored such books as *Mortal Sins, A Full Cup, Fall from Grace, Heaven on Earth,* and many more. He has written for publications, such as *The New York Times Magazine, Esquire,* and *Sports Illustrated.* In one of his more popular books, *The Truth about Trump,* he quotes Mr. Trump's second wife, Marla Maples:

> In one passage she quotes a Trump attorney saying, "Donald is a believer in the big-lie theory. If you say something again and again, people will believe you." In another passage, Maria Brenner (journalist for *Vanity Fair*) had told her, "He was always a phony, and we filled our papers with him." (D'Antonio, Michael. *The Truth about Trump,* Thomas Dunn Books, New York, 2016, p. 216.)

Dr. Robert Jay Lifton has written over twenty books and is a National Books Winner. Two of his popular books are *Death in Life: Survivors of Hiroshima* and *Nazi Doctors.* He has taught at Yale and Harvard Universities and the City University of New York. In my research, I used his book *Losing Reality*. In it, he writes and quotes a journalist, David Leonhardt:

> He is "virtually indifferent to reality, often saying whatever helps him make the case he is trying to make . . . trying to make truth irrelevant . . . Trump's lies are very dangerous as they create a new reality his followers embrace." (Opt. Cit., Lifton, p. 159).

Earlier mentioned, I believe the most seminal work for example of former president Donald Trump's deceit and lying can be found in the written report of The Fact Checkers on the staff at the *Washington Post*. In the introduction of the book, the author Glenn Kessler writes, "This book is not simply a catalogue of false claims; rather, it is a guide to Trump' s attack on the truth. The construction of false but boastful narratives about his achievements is at the core of his political strategy and is a key to his personality" (Kessler, Glenn, (ed). *Donald Trump and the Assault On Truth*, Scribner, New York, p. xii.).

It would be impossible as well as impractical to list the details of the 16,241 lies recorded over the first three years of the Trump presidency. However, to give readers a few examples of this nefarious and outrageous public behavior recorded by *The Washington Post's* Fact Checker team, the following lies are listed.

> "Mexico is paying for the wall. You know that. You'll see that. It's all worked out. Mexico's paying" (Ibid. p. 2).

> "I was the person who saved preexisting conditions in your health insurance" (Jan. 13, 2020), (Ibid., p. 4.).

> "Later on I knew about the payments to Stormy Daniels on an Aug. 23, 2018, Interview" (Ibid., p. 12.).

"I had nothing to do with Stormy Daniels. So she can lie and she can do whatever she wants to do" (Ibid., p.12.).

"Terrible! Just found out that Obama had my wires tapped in Trump Tower just before the victory. Nothing found. This is McCarthyism" March 4, 2017 remarks. (Ibid., p. 17.)!

"I am the least racist person there is anywhere in the world" July 30, 2019, remarks (Ibid., p. 31.).

"It has not been easy for me. As you know I started off in Brooklyn, my father gave me a small loan of a million dollars" (Oct. 26, 2015, remarks). In all, the *Times* found that Trump received the equivalent of at least $413 million in today's dollars from his father's real estate empire (Ibid., p.33.).

"I am the most transparent president in history," Nov. 15,2019, remarks (Ibid., p,43.).

"I'm the only one who tells you the facts" Nov. 3, 2028, campaign rally. (Ibid., p, 46.).

"Take a look outside at the thousands of people that wanted to get inside. You got lucky" (Nov. 15, 2018, rally in Indiana). Reporters looked outside. There was no one (Ibid., p. 77.).

"And we are considered far and away the hottest economy anywhere in the world, not even close."

"I watched in Jersey City, New Jersey, where thousands and thousands were cheering as the buildings (Trade Centers) came down. Trump was attacking Muslims with this statement, and there is no evidence that anything like this took place" (Ibid., p. 17.).

"I was the best baseball player in New York when I was young" (Ibid., p. 17.).

"In addition to winning the electoral college in a landslide, I won the popular vote if you deduct the millions of people who voted illegally" (Ibid., p. 20).

"I haven't had an empty seat at a rally" (Ibid., p. 16.).

Opt. Cit., Sider, "We've decimated Obamacare." Nov. 2, 2018, campaign rally (Opt. Cit., Sider, p. 91.).

Another statement from Ronald J. Sider, (ed) in his 2020 book, *The Spiritual Danger of Donald Trump,* to close this chapter. Dr. Sider is Distinguished Professor emeritus of Theology, Holistic Ministry, and Public Policy, Palmer Theological Seminary at Eastern University.

Trump lies so often that those who know him say he is a pathological liar. Trump's former lawyer, John Dowd, said to him, "You can't tell the truth. You just make things up." Kellyanne Conway was interviewed by Chuck Todd on *I Meet the Press* and asked why Spicer used the first press conference to lie about the size of the inauguration crowd? Conway answered that the White House was providing alternative facts "to counter the mainstream's media inaccurate description of the inauguration." (Opt. Cit., Wehner, p. 113–114)

Our country has never seen a leader as shameless and remorseless as Trump when it comes to lying. Trump is the greatest liar-in-chief our country has ever elected.

And finally, Michael Cohen, who was Special Counsel to President Trump from 2017–2018 and was vice-president of the Trump Organization before then, in his Memoir on the president, *Disloyal,* he wrote, "I would come to understand that questions of right and wrong didn't matter to Trump in the least" (Opt. Cit., Cohen, p. 32.).

Loss of International Credibility

Former president Donald Trump's foreign policy was generated from a sense of grievance—he believed that the United States was being taken advantage of by the other members of NATO, in that they were not paying their fair share of the costs of the protection our country was providing them.

As early as 2016, Trump began his campaign by saying, "I ran for president because I cannot watch this betrayal of our country any longer. I could not sit by as career politicians let other countries take advantage of us on trade, borders, foreign policy and defense" ("Foreign Policy of the Donald Trump administration," en.wikipedia.org/wiki/foreign_policy_of_the_trump_administration#:~;text=u.s.%2).

- On January 23, 2017, three days after taking office, he withdrew from the Trans-Pacific Partnership which he deemed a "job killing partnership."
- In April 6, 2017, the administration reversed the US-Korea Free Trade Agreement, which Trump also described as a job-trading trade deal when he was still a presidential candidate.
- In May 2017, Mr. Trump in a meeting with NATO in Brussels announced that he expected each of them to "finally contribute their fair share" to the alliance. This resulted in $100 billion being committed for the defense of the alliance, for which Trump was given credit.
- In June 2017, the former president announced that he would withdraw the US from the Paris Agreement to combat climate change. The US would be the only country leaving

this organization. Trump simply denied the seriousness of the environmental crisis.

- On June 19, 2018, the UN ambassador Nikki Haley announced that the US would withdraw from the Human Rights Council. She cited the council's chronic bias against Israel and the human rights abuses of various sitting members, including China and Venezuela.

- On May 29, 2020, Trump announced that the US would cease funding of the World Health Organization. His reason was that it had protected China while the coronavirus outbreak spread to other countries. (Ibid., Wikidpeida)

There were other withdrawals, but these were the major instances. At one point when staff were trying to explain about the terms of withdrawal in the various treaties, Trump demanded immediate action. He said, "I don't care about any of this stuff . . . I want it on my desk by Friday" (Opt. Cit., Woodward, p. 156).

The tragedy in Trump's efforts to isolate the US from other nations in order to protect and better serve our nation, actually does just the opposite. There is more strength and protection being part of a union than trying to achieve those goals alone. International law largely exists to promote and protect state sovereignty. As one writer has said, "Trump is a political amateur, always behaving erratically."

Fortunately, when President Joe Biden became president, he reversed Trump's bad foreign policy decisions, but the damage will take years to repair.

Loss of Trust in Government and Democratic Ideals

The subject of this section will best be described by reviewing the comments of other writers who have done in-depth research into the life and thoughts of the former president. They are as follows:

- Michiko Kakutani, a Pulitzer Prize-Winning critic and the former chief book critic for the *New York Times,* who has written. "Truth is the cornerstone of Democracy" in *The Death of Truth* (Opt. Cit., Kakutani, p. 19.).

- George Washington warned "about the rise of cunning, ambitious, and unprincipled men" who might try "to subvert the power of the people" and "usurp for themselves the reins of government, destroying afterwards the very engines which have lifted them to unjust dominion" (Ibid, pp. 169–170).

- The American political system is fundamentally broken—a fact that the Republican Party has ruthlessly exploited to rig politics in their favor (Opt. Cit., Pfeiffer, p. xiv.).

- He (Trump) has changed the language of democracy and its ideals for the language of autocracy. He demands allegiance not to the US Constitution but to himself, and he expects the members of Congress and the judiciary to applaud his policies and wishes" (reference unavailable).

- Two norms are essential to democracy's survival—mutual toleration and institutional forbearance . . . when parties view one another as mortal enemies, the stakes of political competition heighten dramatically (Zablatt, Daniel & Levitsky, Steven; *How Democracies Die,* Penguin Books, USA, 2018, pp. 104, 106.).

- A president's ideal qualities: "A pleasant temperament, virtue, confidence, wisdom, generosity, leadership, compassion, sound and sensible, good character, sense of fairness and justice." Mr. Trump possesses none of these (Meacham, Jon, *The Soul of America,* Random House, New York, 2018, The author is a Pulitzer Prize-biographer, and a contributing writer for *The New York Times Book Review.* pp. 37–47.).

- "Today, the attack on the Constitution is more insidious. The Constitution has remained intact, but the ideas behind it have morphed into a hideous monstrosity encapsulated in the visage of one man, Donald Trump . . . We have entered what could be the worst period in American history unless we do something about it along with other patriots." The author is on the *New York Times* best sellers. He is a globally recognized intelligence community member and a counterterrorism analysis for *NBC News* and MSNBC (Nance, Malcolm. *The Plot to Betray America,* Hachette, New York, 2019. pp. 229–235.).

- The United States presidency may well be the most important and powerful position in the world. Bob Woodward in his book *Fear* describes a dialogue between North Korea's Kim Jung Un and President Trump. It took place on a New Year's Day address by the North Korean dictator who reminded the US. "All of the mainline US is within the range if our nuclear strike." He further reminded the US "that the Nuclear Button is on his desk at all times."

President Trump did not take kindly to that veiled threat and responded, "Will someone from his depleted and starved regime please inform him that I, too, have a Nuclear Button, but it is much bigger and more powerful one than his, and my button works!" Woodward reminds his readers, Trump's retort "played on Kim's insecurities. In the last six years, eighteen of Kim's eighty-six missiles had failed, according to the Center for Nonproliferation Studies" (Woodward, Bob, *Fear,* Simon & Schuster, New York, 2018, pp. 300–301).

The following is a quote from one of Trump's nemesis, Rick Wilson, a seasoned Republican political strategist who has a regular column in *The Daily Beast*—a must-read in the political community. He is a frequent guest on CNN, MSNBC, and NPR. In his book *Everything Trump Touches Dies,* he writes, "I never have to defend a verbally incontinent, psychologically unbalanced, grotesquely ignorant failure who is reviled by his country, mocked by the rest of the world, and who embarrasses himself and the nation with every crude, impulsive act" (Opt. Cit., Wilson, p. 310.).

Loss of Confidence in the Office of the President

"The president himself, absent from any organizational rigor, often acted as his own chief of staff . . . Moreover, his relatives acted as ad hoc general managers of whatever areas they might choose to be general managers in." *Fire and Fury* by Michael Wolfe, who has received numerous awards for his work, including two National Magazine Awards. He is a regular columnist for several magazines and author of six prior books (Wolfe, Michael. *Fire and Fury*, Little, Brown, Great Britain, 2018, p. 110.).

This is an American authoritarian kleptocracy, (leaders stealing from the government) backed by millionaire white nationalists both in the United States and abroad, meant to strip our country down for parts, often using ethnic violence to do so . . . No one holds Trump accountable because he is exactly what he claimed to be railing against an elite billionaire with no concern for the average person (reference unavailable).

"His campaign chair, deputy campaign chair, lawyer, national security advisor, political consigliere, and foreign policy advisor were all found guilty of a potpourri of crimes. Most spent time in prison. His EPA administrator, secretary of the interior and secretary of veteran affairs all resigned in scandal . . . Trump has used the federal government to line his own pockets by directing government spending to his hotels and golf resorts . . . Trump has refused to release his tax returns . . . Trump has gotten away with all of it. The lying, the lawbreaking, the corruption, and the crimes have all gone unpunished. There has been little or no accountability . . . For most of Trump's tenure, his poll numbers have been historically bad" (Opt. Cit., Pfeiffer, pp. 239–240.).

"Trump rejected the better judgment of almost all of his staff. He has done this before. His perverse independence and irrationality ebbed and flowed. But with Charlottesville, the floodgates just opened" (Opt. Cit., Woodward, Page 252.)

"Like a mafia boss, he expected them (his staff) to pledge silence and show allegiance to him over their constitutional duties." (*The Plot to Betray America* by Malcolm Nance, author of *New York Times's* bestsellers and a globally recognized intelligence community member and a counterterrorism analyst for *NBC News*, Page 166.)

Trump Used Military to Extort

"Trump used the specter of military aid to extort the Ukrainian government to investigate Joe Biden . . . His poll numbers had vacillated between mediocre and historically terrible." Pfeiffer was one of Barack Obama's longest-serving advisors (Opt. Cit., Pfeiffer, p. xi.).

"Slavery has been conquered by the Union, but racism lived on across America." *The Soul of America* by Jon Meacham, a Pulitzer Prize-winning author and distinguished professor at Vanderbilt University (Opt. Cit., Meacham, p.58.).

Riot at the Capitol

Trump said, "We're going to have to fight harder . . . You'll never take back our country with weakness, you have to show strength . . . He directed his followers to head to the Capitol building . . . Trump told aids that perhaps Pence should be hanged." (Opt. Cit., Haberman, pp. 481–483.).

The Economy

Former president Donald Trump has boasted many times, taking credit for the strong economy. He claimed the economy in the country was in terrible condition, which he had inherited from President Obama. Quite the contrary was true. Obama had strengthened a poor economy, which was strong at the time that Mr. Trump began his administration.

After his four years in office, he had the following record:

- The economy had lost 2.9 million jobs.
- The trade deficit which he had promised to lower was actually increased by 40.5 percent making the new total almost $7.8 trillion during Trump's time in office.
- The Federal Reserve raised interest rates seven times in 2022.
- Tax cuts did nothing to help the economy but made the rich a lot richer and adding a trillion to the deficit.
- Home prices increased 27.5 percent.
- US-Mexico apprehensions were up 14.7 percent.
- Economic growth rate was down 3.4 percent.
- People without health insurance grew by 3 million.

"Most of the gains have gone to the wealthiest Americans, Wall Street, and the big tech companies, and that is by design. Trump believes that the rich and powerful should get the benefits, not the working and the middle class" (Opt. Cit., Pfeiffer, p. 77.). Also: factcheck.org/2021/10/trumps-final-numbersusafacts.org/state-of-the-union/economy/

Failures

"Many of the deals in *The Art of the Deal* were massive failures—among them the casinos, launch of a league to rival the National Football League, purchase of an airline—but Trump had described each of them a huge successes . . . I never sensed from Trump any guilt or contrition about anything he had done . . . Trump simply didn't traffic in emotions or interest in others . . . His aim is never accuracy; it's dominion" (Opt. Cit., Schwartz, pp. 69–82.).

Trump's Pressure to Get More Votes

"Trump harangued the Georgia secretary of state to find him more votes." To his credit, he did not comply with the president's request. But what he did do was to move the legislature to create a new voting right's package. The rules were strict and made provisions that would prevent such attempted abuse in the future (Opt. Cit., Lemire, p. 216.).

Banning Muslims from Entering the US

"Trump proposed banning all Muslims from entering the US because fears of terrorism." The author, Pfeiffer, was one of Barack Obama's longest serving advisors; he was White House director of communications under President Obama (Opt. Cit., Pfeiffer, p. 33.).

Bankruptcies

"In 1991, the Trump Taj Mahal entered Chapter 11 bankruptcy, the first of his bankruptcies . . . During the fourth bankruptcy case, creditors successfully demanded that Trump get lost . . . In truth, there were actually six bankruptcies" (Opt. Cit., Johnson, p. 93).

Conspiracy Theory and the "Deep State"

Peter Strzok, a Cold War-trained counterintelligence officer said, "Trump is a disaster. I had no idea how destabilizing his presidency would be. The Trump team would seize upon this email and push forward a new conspiracy theory—that the FBI had plotted to overthrow Trump in an illegal coup if he was victorious in his election bid . . . PolitiFac, a political fact-checking website, countered by pointing out that this tweet was not factual . . . He saw a grand conspiracy by the 'Deep State' and he would prove it—by obstructing justice" (Opt. Cit., Nance, pp. 168–169.).

Threats to Individuals

"State secretaries of state came under fire. Georgia's Brad Raffensperger needed security after he refused Trump's demand 'to find' 11,780 votes it would take for the president to flip the state . . . Several armed protesters menacingly stood around Michigan's secretary of state, Jocelyn Benson's home in December 2020 . . . A tweet sent to Colorado secretary of state, Jena Griswold, a Democrat, which read, 'Bullet. That's a six-letter word for you' and 'I'm really jonzing to see your purple face after you've been hanged.' A voice message was left for Arizona secretary of state, Katie Hobbs in September 2020, included this message, which was shared with CNN: 'I am a hunter—and I think you should be hunted. You'll never be safe in Arizona again'" (Opt. Cit., Lemire, p. 211.).

Damage to American Society

"Trump's rageful expressions of xenophobia, racism, sexism, and Islamophobia, experienced the event as traumatic, without quite knowing why . . . In his constant attempts to redefine the truth against wrong-doing he has enacted, Donald Trump behaves like an aggressive perpetrator who fundamentally has no respect for the rights and subjectivities of those in American Society who disagree with him . . . It is heartbreaking to see the damage Donald Trump is wrecking upon American society." "Trauma, Time, and Truth" by Betty P. Ting, LMSW, who is a trauma therapist in the Office of Victim Services of a major hospital in Lower Manhattan, from the book (Opt. Cit., Lee, pp.220–231).

Attempt to Kill the Affordable Care Act

"Mr. President, said Barr jumping in, this case is not going to win. We're in the middle of a COVID epidemic. And you are now creating uncertainty as to people's medical coverage, and you haven't put up a substitute and we're going to lose the case. We knocked out the mandate." Kellyann Conway said, "It was unseemly for the president of the United States to be part of a legal crusade to take away health insurance from 20 million Americans" (Woodward, Bob and Costa, Robert, *Peril*, Simon and Schuster, New York, 2021, pp. 76–77.).

Trump's Losses

"Trump was losing everywhere. Trump and the GOP now have lost more than fifty post-election lawsuits . . . The Supreme Court threw out an effort by congressman Mark Kelly to block the state from certifying the election for Biden . . . Giuliani was the worst—a (expletive) idiot who had gotten Trump impeached . . . Barr wrote a letter of resignation . . . On December 14, the electors in all fifty states and Washington, DC, formally cast their ballots, giving Biden 306 electoral votes, Trump 232" (Ibid., pp. 178, 180.).

Trump's Short-Duration Achievements

"At Trump University, we teach success . . . The faux university did not have professors, not even part-time adjunct professors . . . They were commissioned sales people, many with no experience in real estate . . . The whole Trump University enterprise was a fraud—a scam in which the desperate and the gullible paid about $40 million which turned out to be high-pressure salesmanship . . . The explanation offered by Trump's Foundation will likely induce utter disbelief from people who run charitable foundations or who work in their grant-making departments. It will also raise the eyebrows of any experienced public corruption prosecutor" (Opt. Cit., Johnson, pp. 120, 125.).

"He also tried his hand at aviation . . . He snapped up a fleet of twenty-one ageing Boeing 727s from the struggling carrier at a remarkable modest price of $365 million for the aircraft and landing slots . . . It struggled to thrive economically . . . Trump missed an $1.1 million interest payment in September 1990, the loans were defaulted, and ownership of the airline passed to the bank." By Oliver Smith, "Trump Shuttle: Looking back at Donald Trump's failed, forgotten airline" (shm.com.au/traveller/travel-news/trump-shuttle-looking-back-at-donald-trumps-faited-forgotten-airline-20201001-h1r3q8.html).

"Donald Trump was many things in the business world, including owner of the New Jersey Generals, a Football franchise that played in the upstart United States Football League (USFL) in September 1983 for less than $9 million. Behind the scenes, the league was suffering from more than just unfettered spending. Poor planning and mismanagement had some owners searching for stadium leases, while others ran out of money quickly and couldn't pay their players. Teams were sold, moved to other states, or just discontinued" (sportshistoryweekly.com/stories/donald-trump-usfl-football-hershal-walker-doug-flutie.1122).

"For three seasons, they were the most successful team in the USFL. In 1985, it folded due to financial difficulties caused by antitrust lawsuits against the NFL owners" (esquire.com/news-politics/a41135/Donald-trump-usfl/). Trump is given credit for destroying both the New Jersey Generals and the United States Football League.

CHAPTER 5

SUMMARY

No president is perfect, but are their certain qualities that stand out as absolutely necessary for a presidential candidate to have for qualification? Are there matters that absolutely disqualify a candidate from holding that office?

The Constitution list only three qualifications:

1. Must be a natural born citizen
2. Must be thirty-five years or older.
3. Must be US resident within the US for fourteen years.

A candidate is disqualified for office in the event of a conviction of treason, bribery, or other high crimes and misdemeanors.

Truth is often determined by perception for those who question the nature of reality. This is why it is possible for our Christian leaders and many others to overlook the criminal and immoral behavior of the former president. Many believe Mr. Trump will not be convicted for his crimes because of a "hung-jury" or a mistrial. All it takes is one juror who has misled the jury test for qualification about his Trump support, to hold-out on his conviction decision, for them to be a disqualification for conviction. That is a real possibility due to the determination of Trump supporters to return him to office. Under the right circumstances, justice can be blind, and we live in a culture that has been so brainwashed about Trump's qualifications, that this misguided reality can be possible.

Having established that dangerous possibility, the public must be made aware of the kind of president they really want, and understand the consequences of their choice. Mr. Trump has made it quite clear in his speech and quotations about him, the nature of his goals:

- He will not select members for his cabinet or employees who do not believe the 2020 election results were invalid. In other words, they must believe the election was stolen by Joe Biden. That is in spite of every investigation that the election was proven to be legitimate.

- He will continue to lie in order to create a reality that supports his deranged goals. Does it make any difference that he distorts and embellishes the true facts to support his own reality?

- He will again withdraw the US from foreign treaties and alienate our allies as he supports our enemies. His isolation tactics do not make America great, but subjects it to unimaginable dangers

- He will continue to support white-supremacist groups and disenfranchise minority groups.

- He will continue to build a power-base built upon violence, deceit, and intimidation.

- He will continue to replace leadership with dictatorship.

- Our nation will continue its violence escalation.

- Our nation will become more divided.

- The quality of our collective moral life will lead us more into a secular direction filled with nihilism and confusion because we are losing our soul.

There are many citizens who want something better in our president. Here are a few qualities that transcends the non-standards of our past president:

First, we want a president who has feelings and cares about us above filling his own personal needs.

Second, we want a president who loves this country and is committed to its progress and quality of life.

Third, we want a president who is guided by traditional Judeo-Christian morals and values.

Fourth, we want a president who is a team player and values and uses the opinion and advice of the members of his team. He shares leadership. This style carries over into world politics as he values the association and cooperation with other worldwide democratic leaders and, in so doing, strengthens America's security.

There are many other sterling qualities, such as communication skills, positive attitude, intelligence, good health, knowledgeable, trustworthy, and truthful. He must have a knowledge of history, world affairs, and the Constitution.

This book's title, *What Qualities Does America Want in a President* and the subtitle, *Donald Trump v. Democracy*, appears to line up two choices that are linked to political philosophies, and they are related to our political parties. The Republican Party has morphed into Trumpism—autocracy, authoritarianism, narcissism, unquestioned obedience, and violence. The Democratic Party has maintained its traditional philosophy of freedom, voting rights, citizen participation, justice, tolerance, accountability, economic freedom, Bill of Rights, human rights, and rule of law.

The choice seems like a no-brainer, but there are millions who would choose the route of violence over peace, slavery over freedom, and dictatorship over representative and participatory government. Democracy is not perfect; neither is autocracy. There are injustices and unfairness; more so in totalitarianism.

But there is a compass in the heart of democracy that always points toward improvement. No such compass exists in autocracy—just violence and selfishness. Our forefathers lived under a monarchy with limited freedom. They were not allowed to worship as they felt the guidance of their God. They yearned to breathe freedom's air to the point of risking their lives and property to find a new way. Their compass pointed to a distant land where they could worship their God and govern themselves. The cost was very high but so would be the cost of doing nothing. Their motivation was faith, freedom and self-determination and strong belief that life could be better but they had a choice to make. That choice would affect their future and the future of generations to come. Their choice not only affected them but many others.

America faces a crossroad. The Bible speaks of two roads—the broad way and the narrow way. The conclusion was that the narrow way leads to life (Matt. 7:13). We face ubiquitous choices every day because God created a moral universe beginning with Adam and Eve, who took the wrong road. The beloved poet, Robert Frost, gave us verses about "The Road Not Taken." In it he lists four characteristics about the choices we make every day of our lives:

1. He could not travel both roads.
2. One road was grassy but wanted wear.
3. The choice is irreversible.

4. He took the "one less-traveled" but it has "made all the difference."

In the 2024 presidential election, America will make a choice, and that choice, good or bad, "will make all the difference." Let's hope and pray that it will be a victory for democracy "from sea to shining sea!"

BIBLIOGRAPHY

Books

Applebaum, Anne. *Twilight of Democracy,* Doubleday, New York, 2020.

Blair, Gwenda. *The Trumps: Three generations That Built an Empire.* Simon & Schuster, New York, 2000.

Bolton, John. *The Room Where It Happened,* Simon and Schuster, New York, 2020.

Brockenbrough, Martha. *Unprecedented,* Feiwel and Friends, New York, 2018.

Campbell, John L. *American Discontent: The Rise of Donald Trump and Decline of the Golden Age,* Oxford University Press, New York, 2018.

Cohen, Michael. *Disloyal, A Memoir,* Skyhorse Publishing, New York, 2020.

D'Antonio, Michael. *The Truth about Trump.* Thomas Dunn Books, New York, 2016.

Du Mez, Kristin Kobes. *Jesus and John Wayne,* Liveright Publishing Corporation, New York, 2010.

Gilligan, James. *Violence,* Vintage Books, New York, 1997.

Glass, Leonard. "Should Psychiatrists Refrain From Commenting on Donald Trump's Psychology," in Lee, Brandy, *The Dangerous Case of Donald Trump*, a Thomas Dunn Book, New York, 2017.

Goldberg, Jeffrey (ed). *The American Crisis*, Simon and Schuster, New York, 2020.

Green, Joshua. *Devil's Bargain*, Penguin Press, New York, 2017.

Haberman, Maggie. *Confidence Man*, Penguin Press, New York, 2022.

Hassan, Steven. *The Cult of Trump*. Free Press, New York, 2019.

Howe, Ben. *The Immoral Majority*. Broadside Books, New York, 2019.

Johnson, David Kay. *It's Even Worse Than You Think*, Simon & Schuster, New York, 2018.

Johnson, David Kay. *The Making of Donald Trump*. Melville House, Brooklyn, 2016.

Kakutani, Michiko. *The Death of Truth*, Tim Duggan Books, New York, 2018.

Kendzior, Sarah. *Hiding in Plain Sight*, Flatiron, New York, 2020.

Kessler, Glenn (ed). *Donald Trump and His Assault on Truth*. Scribner.

Lee, Bandy, (ed), *The Dangerous Case of Donald Trump*, A Thomas Dunn Book, New York, 2017.

Lemire, Jonathan. *The Big Lie*, Flatiron Books, New York, 2022.

Levitsky, Steven and Ziblatt, *How Democracies Die*, Broadway Books, New York, 2019.

Lifton, Robert Jay. *Losing Reality*. The New Press, New York, 2019.

Miller, Greg. *The Apprentice*, Custom House, New York, 2018.

Nance, Malcolm. *The Plot to Betray America.* Hachette Books, New York, 2019.

Pfeiffer, Dan. *Un-Trumping America, Twelve, New York, 2020.*

Posner, Sarah. *Unholy.* Random House, New York, 2020.

Rucker, Philip and Leonnig, Carol. *A Very Stable Genius,* Penguin Books, 2021,2022.

Schwarz, Tony. "I wrote the Art of the Deal With Donald Trump," in Lee, Brandy (ed). *The Dangerous Case of Donld Trump,* St. Martin's Press, New York, 2017.

Seat, Leroy. *Fed Up With Fundamentalism.* (Rev), 4-L Publications, 2020.

Sider, Ronald. *The Spiritual* Danger *of Donald Trump. Cascade Books,* Eugene, OR, 2020.

Strzok, Peter. *Compromised,* Houghton, Mifflin, Harcourt, New York, 2020.

Toobin, Jeffrey. *True Crimes and Misdemeanors.* The Bodley Head, London, 2020.

Trump, Mary L. *Too Much and Never Enough. Simon & Schuster, New* York, 2020.

Wehner, Peter. *The Death of Politics,* Harper One, New York, 2019.

Wilson, Rick. *Everything Trump Touches Dies,* Free Press, New York, 2018.

Wolff, Michael. *Fire and Fury,* Little Brown, London, 2018.

Woodward, Bob. *Fear: Trump in the White House,* Simon & Schuster, New York, 2018.

Woodward, Bob and Costa, Robert. *Peril*, Simon & Schuster, New York, 2021

Websites

Paste Magazine, October 22, 2020. pastemagazinecom/politics/donald-trump/donald-trump-so-appealing-to-so-many-people

https://www.businessinsider.com/women-accused-trump-sexual-misconduct-list-2017-12

https://www.washingtonpost.com/politics/trump-recorded-having-extremely-lewd-conversations-about-women-in-2005/2016/10/07/3b9ce776-8cb4-11e6-bf8a-3d26847eeed4_story.html

cnn.com/2022/04/12/us/state-of-the-black-america-voting-report/index.html

democracymatters.org/our-issues/why-we-need-reform

history.com/topics/black-history/slavery

history.com/topics/black-history/civil-rights-movement.

vox.com/2016/7/25/12270880/donald/-trump-racist-racism-history

theledger.com/story/opinion/2022/05/31/shocking-report-reveals-depth-hypocricy-southern-baptist-leaders/9924240002/

barna.com/research/the-end-of-absolutes-Americas-new-moral-code/

Vox.com/22798975/democracy-threats-peril-trump-voting-rights)

bbc.com/news/world-us-canada-48595411.

Reicher, Stephen D. and Haslam, S. Alexander. "Trump's Appeal: What Psychology Tells Us," *Scientific American*, March 1, 2017.

https://www.scientificamerican.com/article/trump-rsquo-s-appeal-what-psychology-tells-u.

https://www.newsmax.com/newsfront/evangelicals-christians-ralph-reed-trump/2019/10/09/id/936344.

Politico journal, 11/19/2020

ancientbiblicalworld.com.8-code-of-hammurabi-moabite-stone/

en.wikipedia.org/wiki/foreign_policy_of_the_trump_administration#:~;text=u.s.%2

factcheck.org/2021/10/trumps-final-numbersusafacts.org/state-of-the-union/economy/

shm.com.au/traveller/travel-news/trump-shuttle-looking-back-at-donald-trumps-faited-forgotten-airline-20201001-h1r3q8.html

sportshistoryweekly.com/stories/donald-trump-usfl-football-hershal-walker-doug-flutie.1122

esquire.com/news-politics/a41135/Donald-trump-usfl/

britannica.com/event/voting-rights-act

en.wikipedia.org/wiki/Trump:_The_Art_of_the_Deal

www.vox.com/2015/9/22/9368591/trump-global-warming

www.ncbi.nlm.nih.gov/pmc/articles/PMC9115435

www.politico.com/story/2015/06/donald-trump-2015-announcement-10-best-lines-119066

INDEX

Printed in the USA
CPSIA information can be obtained
at www.ICGtesting.com
CBHW022210221124
17857CB00046B/424